A BROWN TROUT BICYCLE...

OR

Once Upon the Woods & Waters

By

Ed Gilbert

Order this book online at www.trafford.com
or email orders@trafford.com

Most Trafford titles are also available at major online book retailers.

Printed in the United States of America.

ISBN: 978-1-4907-5318-8 (sc)
ISBN: 978-1-4907-5340-9 (e)

Trafford rev. 12/22/2014

www.trafford.com
North America & international
toll-free: 1 888 232 4444 (USA & Canada)
fax: 812 355 4082

INTRODUCTION

Herein is a collection of but a few of the thousands of short stories and columns written by an 'old-timer' who's had a lifetime of out-of-doors experiences.

The writing is direct and often humorous, expressed in a manner not encumbered by a complicated writing style. It is about adventures, from boyhood into manhood. In simple terms, it is a collection of stories that provide a brief glimpse into the down-to-earth adventures during one man's years in Michigan's outdoor world.

It is a look into a lifestyle that is basically much the same for many people today as it was during my yesteryears. It truly has been a 'Once Upon the Woods & Waters' adventure.

Ed Gilbert

ACKNOWLEDGMENT

My thanks to various newspapers, magazines and other media around the country for publishing many of my stories and columns over the years.

Also, many thanks to those fishers, hunters and other out-of-doors minded folks who have shared some of their stories and adventures with me. Some of those have found their way into my writings although most are from personal experience.

A special thanks must go to Gerry Vandlen and Mary and Gerri Gilbert. Without their assistance this book could not have been published.

Ed Gilbert

Silver Dollars and a Brown Trout Bicycle

Freddie Bradkins was one of those kids born with a silver spoon in his mouth—or it could have been silver dollars in his pockets. Whatever, you know the type—he would never be found fishing, playing sandlot baseball or football, or even swimming with the rest of us guys.

Freddie was always off by himself, usually riding one of his new toys, the latest of which, one summer, was a shiny silver bicycle. His old man was a teller at the only bank in our one-street town. As such, and during the war that raged on at the time, he made more money than most of the other fathers. So he bought Freddie Jr. about everything a boy could ask for.

Well now, I really coveted that shiny, silver bicycle. I was 12 and had never even owned a tricycle, let alone a real bike. So, after admiring that bike over half of that summer, I finally got up nerve enough to ask Freddie if he'd like to sell it.

"Sure," freckle-faced Freddie replied with an arrogant, rabbit-like grin. "It's yours for $20 ... guess you'll never own it then, right?"

It was certain that he knew I hadn't a snowball's chance of ever coming up with a $20 bill, and deep inside, so did I. But Freddie's arrogance really prodded me on, and I became determined to do it.

So I set about mowing lawns and asking neighbors for odd jobs, and as the end of summer became imminent I found I'd amassed a total fortune of $2—way short of the goal.

Ah, but that's when destiny took my hand. Almost every summer evening I'd take my fly rod upstream and fish the creek that flowed down and through my back yard.

On that particular evening I meandered about a half-mile up the creek, where I tied on one of my favorites, a bucktail fly—a real smasher for those native German brown trout.

I'd landed a few small fish but hadn't encountered any "smashing" action when I came to a small backwater area that I'd usually ignored. But that evening I flipped the old wet fly about 30 feet into the backwater next to a burned-out pitch pine stump, and things suddenly got pretty exciting.

It started innocently enough, as a large fish surfaced and merely sucked in the fly. It hardly made a ripple on what was soon to become my lagoon of happiness.

I reared back on the rod and a large brown trout rose up, suddenly feeling the hook. Then it tail-danced on the water several times, something I'd never seen a brownie do before, and seldom since. It ran out another 20 feet of line or so, then turned and swam straight at me. I looked down at the monster, in awe as the 10-pound-class trophy actually swam straight between my legs. I suddenly wished I'd at least have brought my net along—could have netted it right there!

I played that fish nearly an hour before being able to pull it in to the stream bank. Then, as I lifted it up and out of the water, I found myself gazing directly into the face of an elderly gentleman. He was decked out in a black suit, with tie and hat, and stared back and forth between me and that monster trout. Thinking back, I almost believe he was salivating.

"Son," he remarked with a wide grin, "tell you what. I'll give you a $10 bill for that fish."

At first my mind went crazy at the thought of such an outrageous fortune as $10. Then I glanced at the fish again, the largest brown trout I'd ever landed. My parents would be very proud to see I'd caught such a monster.

Then suddenly that silver bicycle flashed to mind. Why, with this man's 10-spot I'd have $12—over half way to getting that bike! So the next thing I knew I'd handed over that brown trout and was holding a crisp $10 bill.

Yes, I told mom and dad what had happened. They knew I'd been saving for that bicycle, so with a slight expression of regret at not seeing the trophy, they said they supposed I'd made a good deal.

Then suddenly the brilliant idea surfaced, as my dad remarked, "That $10 bill's as good as gold—well, maybe not gold, but you can trade it for 10 silver dollars at the bank."

Flash as a rat the idea was there! At the bank! That was it! My mind was clicking like a cash register.

So the next day I marched into the local stronghold with the $10 bill and my two ones—$12 in all, and up to the teller at the window. It was Freddie's dad!

"May I help you, young man ?" He stared down at me almost as though I were a bug or something.

"Yes, sir," I blurted out. "I'd like to get 12 silver dollars for these bills." I was nervous as a cat in the middle of a dance floor during a jitterbug contest.

Well, Freddie's dad counted out 12 silver, 'walking liberties,' and I plunked them into an overall pocket. Then I marched out of there, with a starboard list from all that weight and an ear-to-ear grin on my kisser. Everything was going according to plan.

That same afternoon I spotted Freddie. He was downtown, sitting on that silver bike and sucking up a butter pecan ice cream cone in front of Mac's Ice Cream Parlor. I sauntered up to freckle-faced Freddie.

"Tell you what," I remarked casually, "I've got something in my pocket I'm going to trade you for that bike."

Freddie's eyebrows went up. I'd caught his attention. "Oh yeah? What's that?"

"I've got 12 real silver dollars here, and I'll trade 'em for that bike."

Freddie's eyes widened as I pulled out the silver coins and handed them to him.

"Deal?" I asked hesitantly.

"Deal!" said Freddie. So he handed over the bike and headed off to the bank where he would tell his dad, the teller, what a grand deal he'd just made.

Well now, I didn't wait around. I jumped on that bike and peddled like heck for home, a half-mile out of town and hopefully too far to hear Freddie's old man chew him out for being such a sucker.

Of course I expected repercussions to occur over the incident, but none ever came. Freddie never mentioned it again, and neither did I.

But many times thereafter did I thank that 10-pound German brown trout for being where it was on that August evening.

I was 16 when I finagled to buy my first car...ah, but that's another story. And, as you may guess, I didn't buy it from Freddie!

'No Man's Island'—One Remembered

I reckon that somewhere in everyone's life there is a 'No Man's Island' of one sort or another—a place we'll always retain as a fond memory.

My 'island' is located in the middle of a trout stream in west-central Michigan.

When I was at the formidable age of 9 our family relocated from the Petoskey area to a more central part of the state, the move dictated by my father's advancement in the (then) Conservation Department. Moving from a rural area to somewhat of another, the change didn't leave many outdoor activities in the dust, as our new home stood among several trout ponds while the Pere Marquette River twisted along not 50 paces from my bedroom window.

At first my young and adventuresome friends from Petoskey were sorely missed, but it wasn't long before new faces and friendships made the old ones get somewhat fuzzy and more difficult to recall.

The first new faces to come floating along the river, on old inner-tubes, were Jack and Tom McLenithan, brothers who lived about a half-mile distant. And one day along came Sam Avery, a near-neighbor who would eventually become a buddy for many years thereafter.

We played rough games together, and in those games it became natural that Sam and I'd pair off against the brothers. For it was soon evident that you didn't fight or even argue with a brother's own brother—if you did, the other brother would quickly turn on you, and suddenly there you'd be, fighting three guys rather than two!

Some distance downstream from our home the PM River had years before split apart to form an island—not large, maybe 80 feet in length by about 50 or so wide. And this was the island that was soon to become more like a kingdom in itself—we sort of grew up there.

At first we treated the island as joint ownership, the four of us sharing it for camping out and as a fishing base. But that circumstance wore thin, as did the first summer, and we were to discover that fighting for possession of the island was much more interesting—and perhaps just dangerous enough to add more excitement to our lives.

So Jack and Tom paired off against Sam and me, and our island got its name—No Man's Island. It was to belong to whoever possessed it at any given time. Our mock battles with wooden swords and toy cap pistols caused that real estate to change ownership often—almost on a daily basis.

Actually, our action was not unlike that old 'capture the flag' game. But it soon became more intense, for while staging attacks on each other's kingdom we added a rather dangerous item to our arsenal.

The four of us each owned a Red Ryder BB gun, and we discovered that a BB, if only fired at another's backside, would sting while not leaving any permanent damage. (A warning to any youngsters who may read this story: do not try this today, as BB guns or others of the pellet variety marketed now are capable of much higher velocity and may penetrate the skin or perhaps even kill!)

Our wild warfare waged on through several summers, sometimes extending into the nights when I'd quietly sneak out my bedroom window to meet Sam. Then we'd in turn sneak up on and attack Jack and Tom on the island. But here there was a difference, as guns were ruled out at night because no one could tell the front from the rear of another—especially of a moving target.

But that fall a distant event changed our thinking concerning the use of BB guns. I received word that one of my old friends up in Petoskey had lost an eye from a BB gunshot, and upon informing the others of such, it was agreed that henceforth the only guns we'd use were our old western cap pistols.

So gradually, perhaps due to the removal of the past danger element of BB guns, or even more so that we were now several summers older, we once again began to share No Man's Island.

During the following two summers the four of us camped out on the island nearly every night. Sometimes, we'd even rig up set lines, which were illegal, and enjoy a tasty breakfast of rainbow or brown trout.

The regular trout season opened then as it does now, on the last Saturday of April, and on two of those openers we set up a hot chili and coffee stand on the island, from which we industriously sold the stuff at 15 cents per item to passing fishermen. This proved a profitable venture that allowed us to purchase a fine tent, along with cooking pots and other camping gear… So, No Man's Island continued to live on and to thrive.

We swam at the island during the summers. There was a deep hole at the downstream end, and above it a large tree from which we rigged a rope that enabled us to swing out over the hole in Tarzan fashion and fling ourselves downward while thumping our chests and yelling madly.

Many times we did this in our birthday suits, but that ended abruptly one afternoon when we heard tee-hee's up on the bank and looked up to discover a troop of Girl Scouts pointing and jumping about with laughter—their leader attempting to turn them about and spirit them away!

But time and tide do not wait, and with many summer adventures we gradually grew up—and I don't recall just when—to eventually abandon the enchantment of our island kingdom and move on with our lives.

I still think of that island occasionally, and have even returned to fish there over the years … oh yes, it still exists. It exists to me, as I'm certain it does to Jack, Tom and Sam. For it was much more than just a tangle of land and trees in the middle of a river—it was part of our adventuresome youth, and ultimately, an important reflection on the mirror of our lives.

Fishing Long Ago and Far Away

As a lad I lived by a river that meandered through my father's trout ponds, and there I spent my early youth believing that all people were created for a singular purpose—to fish.

Not until my teens was I to discover that we were also created to hunt, and by then fishing was so ingrained within me that it would always remain my preference of the two outdoor activities.

My father, an employee of the Conservation Department (now DNR), had charge of 18 trout-rearing ponds and, of course, the river that wound a path through them.

The location and everything about it was fascinating to a kid, including my father's several employees who helped with the feeding and care of thousands of rainbow, brook and brown trout. There was "Doc" Fisher, a small, wiry man with an apt last name, except that I never knew him to fish. And Arthur was a man with but one arm, his right one, yet capable of doing anything the others could. Then there was "Scottie," a wise-cracking, hard-working guy whose ancestry was as obvious as his wit.

Those three individuals formed an unforgettable picture indeed for a youngster, and I became so engrossed in their work that I spent many hours helping them to feed or count fish, clean ponds, pick out dead fish, and, I suppose now, making a general nuisance of myself.

But I also began to fish in the river, and to say frequently would be an understatement. I was in the stream day and night, and I guess could even bear witness to that old joke, "I once caught a fish in my pajamas—how it got in my pajamas I'll never know!"

I fished alone early on, much as I often do these days. However, after my first season of drowning crawlers with a near-zero success rate, something happened that enlightened me.

I was on one of my bait-drowning benders when two neighbor boys happened along. They both scoffed at my can of sticky worms, immediately charging me with being an idiot. However, they then explained that since the fish in the ponds were being fed ground liver and horsemeat, some of the stuff filtered its way into the river itself so fish in the river were used to eating the same.

It was an awakening moment. I ran immediately to my dad's walk-in cooler, where the large cans of fish food were stored, placed a quantity of the stuff in a soup can and beat a path back to the river.

Ah, success was mine! Within a couple hours I landed my limit of dandy rainbow and brown trout, 20 being the limit at the time.

Such fine catches were repeated often during that summer, mom being especially pleased as a war was on and the fish were fine table fare. With dad it was a different story. He thought it was OK, but wouldn't it be more sportsmanlike to angle in a traditional manner rather than stick a gob of horsemeat on a hook.

Dad eventually won out, and I came to realize that it was actually more exciting to outsmart a fish with a fly rod and homemade flies. Thereafter, I never used the 'greasy kid stuff.'

Ask any of us 'old timers' about learning to fish. We'll all have stories to tell you. Which leads me to the reason for writin' this old fish story.

To me, fishing isn't merely a sport or pastime. It's an institution. And I can think of no singular item that brings more thought and focal attention to a youngster than quality time along a river or a lake, fishing rod in hand and the anticipation of landing a fish.

If one desires to teach children the real lessons of life—winning, losing, patience and peacefulness of mind, take 'em fishing. And often. Believe me, they'll return to it later on in life as well.

Yes, for me it was a long time ago in a county far, far away, (if George Lucas will forgive my pun). But it seems like only yesterday that I was wandering the banks of that river, sometimes barefoot, but as happy as the old proverbial lark. And yes, I sometimes return there to fish, but often as not to simply contemplate the lessons the place instilled in me as a youngster, beginning to grow up and to appreciate what fishing and life is all about.

Fishing or Not,
Support Your Local Sheriff

There was a faint crack of brush in the nearby woods, so the four of us stood quietly at our spring campsite near Whopper Lake, peering in that general direction.

Deer, probably moving down to the lake for an evening drink, or so we thought. But then a figure slowly began moving from the wooded area toward the lake, glancing to each side and to the rear as it moved carefully along. It was a man carrying a fishing rod and net, and it appeared that he had purposely blackened his face.

"Hey..." Tom started to say. But he was quickly thwarted as his brother, Jack, clamped a hand over his mouth.

"Quiet," said Jack, the oldest member of our young gang. "Let's see what he's up to. He obviously knows the fishing season hasn't opened yet."

"Yeah," Sam whispered. "He's put charcoal on his face. Looks like a violator, or at least thinks he is."

"You know," I said, "That guy looks familiar to me. What you think, Jack?" Jack suddenly uttered a low laugh.

"I know who that is, and I can hardly believe it," he said. Tom, Sam and I all glanced at Jack. "Who?" came out in unison.

"Well," whispered Jack through a wide grin. "If I'm not mistaken that's the sheriff of this county. Keep quiet and don't move. Let's just watch."

And we four weekend-camper-kids did just that. We looked on as the sheriff of our northern Michigan County sneaked down to the water's edge. And there, after removing his shoes, he carefully waded into the water.

We could hardly contain our joy and laughter as we watched our fearless sheriff thread what looked to be a night crawler onto his hook and cast out over the drop-off.

So we stood in secrecy for about 20 minutes, whispering and caught up in the moment as our lawman landed four dandy bass and stuffed them in a gunny sack. Then, as he ended his illegal fishing and began to put his shoes back on, Jack motioned us to follow along, saying he'd do the talking if any was to be done. So we four lads walked quietly down toward the lakeside. Then, as the man turned to leave, there we stood in his path.

"Hi, mister," Jack said amiably. "Have any luck?"

"Not much," came a rather gruff reply, as the guy, looking a little flustered, kept his darkened face down and moved on by us. "A little early, I guess."

"A whole lot early," remarked Jack. "Maybe we'll give it a try too—later on."

""Go ahead. It's a big lake," came the muffled reply as the figure shuffled off into the woods and out of sight.

When he'd gone, Sam said excitedly, "That sure was ol' Bob! Pretty clever of him, eh?"

"That was him, our own sheriff, and we'd better not say anything about this to anyone," advised Jack. "Could mean some real trouble 'cause he knows who we are too."

So we swore ourselves to secrecy and never did tell anyone—until now, that is.

However, this I will admit. We four pulled some rather shifty shenanigans ourselves after that, and during our high school years. Oh, I wouldn't say we terrorized our little village, nothing that even came close. But we did attack a considerable number of lakes and trout streams while doing a little off-season fishing of our own.

And we were certain that Sheriff Bob knew about some of those times. We were always certain he was even watching us. But we hadn't told on him so I guess he decided not to turn us in. We grew to like and even admire ol' Sheriff Bob over those years of adventure. It's funny how things long forgotten will suddenly pop to mind. This little episode did while I was shuffling through the slush ice on a semi-frozen lake the other day. No one was pulling up much of anything that day—not even an old boot or rusty can.

But I did. I pulled up an old memory, a memory about being carefree rascals who were growing up, and about an old-time sheriff who was also a bit of a rascal. Makes me wonder if there are any left in this world like him...Yes, I hope so!

Thanks kid,
the fish were great, once I got past the sawdust!

The Ice House Caper

Anyone who fishes knows that fish need to be cleaned as soon as possible and kept on ice, or frozen…unless an immediate fish fry is on the program.

I want to tell you about an incident where the kept-on-ice thing became of paramount importance, yet almost impossible.

When I was young, my father had several trout ponds containing thousands of rainbow, brown and brook trout. In order to feed them, we had a large walk-in, cork-lined freezer in our walkout basement. The freezer contained large, heavy cans of ground meat, the fare of the time for growing trout.

I often kept my catch of trout in that freezer too, especially when mom's refrigerator wouldn't hold them all…ahem.

As it was, there was a corner store in our little hamlet that also had cold storage. It was an old-fashioned ice house, where large and small blocks of ice were stored amid piles of sawdust to keep them from melting. That was how they kept ice in those days.

I knew about the ice house because it was located just three blocks from our school, and on hot days several pals and I would sneak in there to cool off. Once in a while we even took girls into the ice house, but since cooling them off was not the object it never seemed to work out. Sometimes its owner, Ol' Man Feathers, would discover us in there and toss us off the premises.

Well, one summer when the temperature was in the 90s, someone ran a truck into a local power pole and the entire town's electricity was fizzled for three days. It was a real crisis. Mom almost went into a fit and became so beside herself it seems like there were two of her.

"Our power may be off for days," she wailed, "and look at all this meat in our refrigerator. It's sure to spoil."

"What about Dad's fish food downstairs and my fish in your fridge?" I asked. "It's all a goner too."

"No," she replied. "The fish food will keep but the other meat up here and your fish won't."

Well, I guess I was at the age where "other meat" such as venison and beef concerned me not. But by my count I had 23 rainbow and brown trout in Mom's freezer compartment, and the thought of losing that was a catastrophe.

I wandered outside to think and suddenly the answer came—the idea that would save my fish and Mom's other meat. The ice house behind Feather's store! It would probably do the trick, at least for a few days. But knowing that Mom would never approve of invading that ice house, I didn't tell her my plan right away. No, I'd at least wait until she discovered her meat and my fish had disappeared.

That evening I bicycled over to my pal Sam's house and secretly explained my idea. He said his mother had the same problem, particularly because of a box of frozen venison. We decided to risk it.

Late that night we each sneaked out of our homes with boxes and packages of goods that we pulled in small wagons. Then we pulled the wagons with our bicycles the half mile to the ice house, quietly opened the door which was never locked, flicked on our flashlights and took the goods inside.

It was necessary to relocate several of the larger ice blocks to hide our goods, but we did so and then covered them with smaller blocks of ice and lots of sawdust. Our plan appeared to have worked perfectly up to then, and we hadn't been noticed even though a jukebox rang out and people were coming and going from a nearby tavern.

We went home laughing and quite pleased with ourselves. But our mothers were all over us the following morning about the missing items from their refrigerators. However, Sam and I had sworn not to tell right away. We'd hold off that day, perhaps for two days or more.

Luckily, I guess, the electricity came back on the evening of the third day, so Sam and I sneaked out again and quietly retrieved our treasures. We got the goods home, scraped off most of the sawdust, and restocked the fridges. We were home free with our caper, but I made a huge discovery when repacking my fish. A package of five of my largest and most beautiful rainbow trout was missing.

There could be but one answer to the missing fish—someone had discovered our caper and helped themselves to my best trout.

Who would do such a thing?

Well, the answer came the following morning. While biking around town I happened to pass the ice house. (One always returns to the scene of the crime, right?) There stood Ol' Man Feathers, and he hailed me to say, "Thanks for the fish, kid. They tasted fine once I got past the sawdust."

It was like, well sort of, a frozen moment in time, and I believe I said something like, "You're entirely welcome!"

And that was the last time any of us kids ever went near the old ice house.

The bike picked up speed at a tremendous rate!

It Was an Awesome Ride

The ski lodges are gearing up for downhill and cross-country skiing now, I see snowmobiles whipping around out on the road, and perhaps some good ice fishing is also on the way. So I guess winter is finally here, and good things are happening in our winter wonderland.

Ah, but what was that? I just saw a kid flashing by in the ice and snow, and on a bicycle? I don't know how he can do that without slip-sliding away.

I don't know what's keeping him upright, but seeing him has suddenly changed my mind about today's column. Rather than writing about ice fishing, which I actually sat down to do, that youngster's activity on a bike has jarred my memory back to when I myself was a kid growing up near the city of Petoskey.

Back in those days I often visited some shirt-tail relation that had a farm above a steep, long hill where the road eventually ended down at Crooked Lake. Many times during the summer months, I and the two brothers, Bobbie and Tom Ulrich, would load up our bikes with fishing gear and walk the bikes down the steep hill to the lake, where we'd fish for bass and northern pike.

Now, this steep hill was, and still is, about a mile long. We always figured it impossible to ride our bikes down it, as it was also rutted and had lots of loose gravel—not really a safe venture.

However, one sunny morning, after loading our bikes with fishing gear, we arrived at the top of that hill and had just got off the bicycles to walk 'em down when Bobbie glanced slyly in my direction and proclaimed, "I'll bet you're too chicken to ride down rather than walk."

As Tom piped in with, "Come on, I dare you to try it," my temper and rise in adrenaline got the better of me.

"OK," I said. "I'll just do it!"

Then, before I could move, Bobbie remarked, "Your bike may be too old for the run. Here, take mine instead." Then he turned over his bike and shot a grin toward his brother.

Not yet aware that I was being set up, I jumped on the bike and yelled, "Here goes nothin'!" and pushed off down the grade.

Well now, the first hundred feet or so wasn't bad, but then the bike began to really pick up speed and I thought I'd better try the brake.

Brake? The bike had none! And then, fully realizing I'd been had, all I could do was attempt to steer around the ruts, miss some of the larger stones, and hold on in total fright as I and the bike continued to pick up speed.

"You dirty rats!" is all I could think of as I soon realized I must be going 50 miles per hour or more and that my life was now totally in God's hands!

I don't know just how, but somehow I and that bike stayed upright down that mile ride, and as the hill began to level off I was finally able to drag my feet and slow it down. The ride ended just before I was about to get dunked in Crooked Lake.

I laid the bike down and sat down, shaking in my shoes, and it was about a half hour before I looked up to see Bobbie and Tom approaching and cheering.

The boys declared that it had been an awesome ride and exciting to see, and Bobbie even apologized for having deceived me into riding his brakeless bicycle.

Yeah, it had been exciting for them to see, but I still wasn't thrilled about the whole adventure. I was really nonplussed, but I did get back at 'em that day by catching twice as many fish as either of them.

You know, I've driven up and down that same hill many times since, and each time been reminded of that day when I was a kid and performed that crazy stunt.

Well, I just looked out the window above my computer again, and there goes that kid in another direction, on his bike and in the ice and snow. He certainly has some deering-do…Wish I still had some!

One Hot Fourth of July,
and a Guy Named Joe

I have a vivid recollection of one very hot July 4.

I worked for the U.S. Forest Service for two summers while still in high school, and I, along with about a dozen other young men (actually, we were boys at the time), was hired by the Baldwin, Mich. ranger station. Our primary duty was to fight forest fires within the Manistee National Forest.

Each morning we'd raise Old Glory over the ranger station and then go about our duties. Although never one to wrap a flag about me and go parading about, I'd learned early on to respect America's flag. But before this day was out, and the three days to follow, I was to wonder several times if I'd ever see Old Glory raised again.

Yes, we were on duty that Fourth of July, as it was a summer with daily temperatures in the 90s and forest fires were rampant throughout the dry woods.

So, fighting fires was our primary duty. But there was a secondary job, equally as tiring. On this day we were to continue the secondary job—that of working in the young pine plantations.

Each man had an axe that he was encouraged to keep razor sharp, and the 12 or so of us would grab our axes and stretch out in a straight line. We walked through the plantations "girdling" (cutting out a ring of bark) the larger trees so they would eventually die off leaving the young pines to grow faster and straighter.

Joe Mack, many years a forester, was our crew chief. He was in charge of us whether fighting fires or working the plantations. Joe was a heavyset, muscular man whose look reminded one somewhat of an eagle coming in for a landing on your head. But Joe was as fair as he was tough, and we all respected him. He was an avid hunter and fisherman as well as being at home as a forester, and most of all he kept things rolling along with jokes and pranks.

One of Joe's favorite tricks was to stand over a nest of yellow jacket bees and to call one of the new boys over to talk to him. Now, yellow jackets build nests in the ground, and upon being disturbed can become the nastiest little critters around. Every so often you'd hear a yelp and see some guy go waltzing off over the trees and stumps with a trail of yellow jackets close on his tail. Of course, when Joe pulled his prank he'd swear later that he never got stung. Well, the other hapless fellow always did. We never really believed Joe, but he always appeared as though unscathed.

Another favorite of Joe's was to tell a new crewman about the "Henaway" he'd just bought, and when the unsuspecting fellow would finally ask, "What's a Henaway?," he'd reply, "Oh, about three, or four pounds, I'd guess!"

On that particular July 4 we'd bounced out in our truck to a plantation about 20 miles from the station, and had worked the woods about a quarter of a mile when Joe came charging through the brush yelling "Fire! Fire!"

We had no such thing as a drill, so we knew it was the real thing. It became a race back to our truck, where we flung ourselves and the axes in and went bouncing off toward the fire area, with Joe at the wheel.

About then most of us, even the seasoned ones, got pretty scared. On a hot and windy day such as this we figured it was going to be a hum-dinger. It was, and we could smell the smoke and see it when several miles away.

This fire had started about five miles west of Wolf Lake, in Lake County, and Joe yelled back from his driver's seat to tell us that it had already burned off a good many square miles.

We unloaded about a half mile east of what was to become our fire line, where we exchanged our axes for "Indian" pumpers. We called them that because you strapped them on your back like a papoose. They weighed about 80 pounds when full of water, and had a pumping hose and nozzle you worked by hand pressure.

Our crew was soon joined by several others, and we strung out in that same straight line we used for girdling trees and headed through the woods. Joe's voice was booming directions from the middle of the pack. The weight of the pumpers and the smoke inhalation combined to nearly do some of us in before we reached the fire.

Then, there it was, snapping and crackling its way toward us at an alarming pace. Sped on by the winds, it could be seen flashing in "top fires" up high in some of the trees, while older trees were literally falling over in its wake.

Now, I'm certain that forest fire fighting is done today with much more sophistication and in a safer manner, but in those days I don't recall that we ever wore masks or really had much protection of any sort. In fact, many of us weren't even wearing shirts.

Shortly, we reached a point where the Forest Service plow had already gone through in an attempt to make a wide and deep enough rut to help hold up the fire. This rut became our fire line, and our job was to try to stop the fire from jumping that ditch.

As the flames and smoke picked up, it became next to impossible to see or hear the men near you, although we were supposed to be about 12 paces from one another. We worked the pumpers though, and did all we could to keep the flames from jumping beyond us. But it became an impossible task. The wind and top fires spread it so we became nearly surrounded by flames, and suddenly Joe's booming voice came through the din, "Fall back! Fall back!"

It was at about that time I recall a loud, cracking sound, and looked up to see an old oak tree coming over at me. Its main trunk was off to my right, but its upper branches were wide, on fire, and I wasn't able to jump fast enough or far enough to totally escape. I wasn't knocked out, just stunned. But I probably would have "bought the farm" as the saying goes. Then suddenly, Joe's eagle-like face was peering down at me. He'd retreated some, saw I was missing, and returned for me.

Joe helped me out of the pumper straps and we let the thing lay. Then he lifted me up and the two of us, nearly overcome by the stifling smoke, wove a scrambled path back to the truck and safety.

We were to fight that fire three more sweltering days.

Some years ago I attended Joe's funeral. He had 30 years in the U.S.F.S., and lived in Hesperia, Mich.

But that 4th of July is one I shall never forget, and although I've had several 'heroes' during my lifetime, Joe Mack is near the top of the list. He will always be there.

"Smelt Are Tasty,
but Really Hard to Scale!"

Smelt dipping in feeder creeks is somewhat akin to sucker spearing, although one doesn't use a spear to get smelt or even use one to spear oneself in the foot, as did a fishing companion of mine a few years ago.

No. Dipping with a net is generally the preferred method for gathering up those silver, tasty darts.

The spring smelt runs are dictated by water temperature. From mid-April onward for a few weeks, as the water temperature increases along the Lake Michigan shoreline, smelt school up in feeder streams to spawn. This usually happens when the water is 40-43 degrees. It has been a little on the chilly side thus far this spring, but April is here and action can't be long in coming.

While still at an early age and growing up in the Petoskey area, I'd sometimes tag along with my dad and two older brothers. They had smelt dipping down to a science. When we spotted a school of smelt, one brother would wade into the creek either above or below the school and scare 'em either down or up to where the rest of us waited, dip nets in hand.

Many times we filled several buckets and a washtub with the little darts and headed for home, all of us smelling as though we'd spent all night in a salmon cannery. Mom wouldn't even let us in the door, telling us to clean them on the back porch.

Of course, cleaning the little rascals was easy, even though there were so many. All one really required then, and is the case yet today, was a pair of scissors to lop off their heads and cut 'em down the middle to gut them.

Yet, with so many, it took many hours.

And, importantly, it wasn't even necessary to scale the fish, as is a necessity with so many other species.

Ah, but I vividly recall one time when we invited a neighbor to go along on one of our smelt-dipping nights. He'd never dipped for smelt before, and when we were loaded to the gills with the little rascals, he didn't even want to take any home with him. Dad finally talked him into taking a pail full, and he stopped in at our house the next day.

Dad asked him how he liked the smelt, upon which Mr. Alvrey replied, "They're very tasty, but really hard to scale!" I guess until that moment no one had told him scaling wasn't required. But when we broke the news to him, his face turned red and he left in a hurry.

It has been several years since I last dipped smelt, and I believe that was the time I cast a net off the pier of Ludington, not in a feeder creek. But I still remember the many good times my brothers, and my dad and I had while floundering around in those little feeder creeks after silver minnows.

I also remember mom standing in the doorway of that old farmhouse and telling us, "You keep those smelly things outside until they're cleaned. Then I want you to take half of 'em and give 'em to the neighbors. My old ice box will only hold so many!" Then she'd retreat inside muttering to herself, "They never learn. I need to retrain 'em every year!"

Now that I've told all this, I'm suddenly getting the bug again... Anyone for some good old-fashioned smelt dipping?

Winter Fun at School

From my picture window in my home office I can see a grade school in the distance. And just now, in that school yard, young kids are frolicking about in the 15-degree temperature. They're building snow forts and snowmen, and the cold weather doesn't seem to phase them at all.

Ah yes, I was once their age and like them, as I recall. So were my buddies. When we were kids, the weather didn't rule our lives. We ruled the weather.

No matter the cold, extreme heat, rain, lightning or whatever nature had in store, we fired right back at it.

Glancing at the school again, I now can see several youngsters on the swings, going high in the air to leap forward and out into the snow. We did that too.

But seeing those kids swinging does bring back the memory of an experience I once had. I believe I was in the third grade. It was winter and most of us were outside for recess.

Well, I took to a swing and began to swing higher and higher. And then I noticed two girls standing out in front of me and watching. They would giggle and point at me quite often, and I was thrilled, thinking they were observing my prowess and deering-do. But the bell suddenly rang to end recess, and I went inside to discover that the fly on my trousers had been unzipped all the while.

Well, the unzipped zipper incident never came up, and I avoided both of those girls like the plague until I took one of them to the senior prom. We didn't discuss it then, either.

Although I see no such thing taking place just now at the school I see through my window, I recall that another popular winter recess event took place when we were kids. That was softball. Yep, we actually played softball in the snow, and used a real ball rather than snow.

But I do recall one softball game we played that almost ended the game for us. My sister was up to bat and I was pitching. I tossed the ball, my sister swung and missed, but the bat went around and struck the girl who was catching squarely in the mouth. The result was that she lost several front teeth and was hurried off to a doctor's office.

There was some anxiety in our house for several months following that incident, as that girl's father just happened to be one of the coaches of the Detroit Tigers! But no reprisals came, and of course we all felt sorry for Heather (I'll not give her last name herein). We all wished her the best when she moved away that following spring.

Now I can see kids sliding on an ice patch over at the school. That reminds me of the winters when our school's janitor flooded a tennis court to make a skating rink. Some just skated, but many of us played hockey. Real hockey sticks were rare items, but we normally beat each other up with sticks carved from tree limbs. But it was fun.

Well, it was a little trip down Memory Lane. But the kids have gone inside the school now, and I guess I should get busy and write a story.

Finding and Losing
the 'Lost Lake' Bonanza

The ice was off the lakes, the bullfrogs were croaking, and bass were swirling about, chasing their prey along the shores of the many lakes within Michigan's Lake County.

Located in the north-central part of the state, Lake County has always boasted 47 trout streams and 156 lakes.

And it is where our family relocated when my father was transferred from Petoskey by the (then) Conservation Department.

It was like an outdoor Heaven to a young boy growing up, and I took advantage of it.

And several years passed. I was still in high school, but working summers at the U.S. Ranger Station for the Forest Service. One day, while going over some old topographic aerial photos of the county, I spotted two little black dots up in a corner of a map. They were obviously either ponds or small lakes.

Until then, I'd believed that my father and I'd fished almost every lake in the county. But here was something new and in an area we hadn't been before.

Then, looking very closely at the two dots, I found no nearby structures and that the only road appearing on the area was a two-track that culminated about a mile away. The rest of the entire area was forest.

It was an exciting moment. I laid my plans carefully and told no one of the discovery. Then, early one Saturday morning I loaded up our old World War II vintage jeep with fishing gear and some sandwiches and headed out, a folded copy of the photo-map in a pocket.

After nearly an hour of wheeling the Jeep down various old, two-rutted logging trails, I finally arrived at a dead end, somewhat resembling the place on the map.

Then, taking along my Bristol, steel telescopic fly rod along with a packet of flies and a rucksack with some sandwiches and other gear, I checked my compass and struck out northwest.

The hike was somewhat desolate yet exciting. There were no trails except those made by deer and other wildlife—no sign that anyone had been there since the Indians had ruled the area.

About three-quarters of a mile into the woods I walked up a rise that looked down upon what had once been a small pond. But it was dead now, and choked with tall grass and brush.

My heart sank a little, and then I thought of that second dot on the aerial photograph. I unfolded the map, spotted it, and hiked around the desolate area to yet another rise. Suddenly there it was, not a hundred yards away, about two acres in size and looking as pristine as those lakes you see in fancy post cards.

I hurried to the side of the pond and hiked around its circumference. There appeared none of the signs that anyone had ever fished it or even been there in the recent past—no old bottles, cans or tangles of monofilament line—nothing but a few deer tracks and those of raccoons that had come to the water's edge.

Then I looked to my fishing tackle, and with but a single cast of an old bucktail fly, a 2-pound bass rose and slammed it. Thus, I landed the first of at least 15 fish I caught and released that morning.

It was like finding a bonanza! Heaven on earth and the fulfilled dream of having your own enchanted fishing pond!

From that day forward, the only person I ever told about the pond was my father, and the two of us went there to fish several times that summer and during the following year.

However, I then took my senior trip to a far-off land with the Marine Corps, returning three years later with a dream of returning to my old, secret, enchanted pond. But when I returned to the pond I was shocked and angered to discover a beaten path in, and at the pond-side many old pop and beer cans along with foam cups scattered about among deserted lunch sacks.

My dream was shattered as I hiked out with a net filled with litter, and later on to discover that another young lad who'd also worked for the U.S. Forest Service had also made the same discovery and hadn't been very secretive about it. Perhaps I had years before circled those two little dots on the map. I don't know.

So there it is. My "bonanza" had become a "banana," so to speak, and I never returned to the pond again. So I suppose after all's said and done, those old words by Pogo are correct: "We have found the enemy, and he is us."

Boats and 'Smitty the Boat Man'

"Smitty the boat man?" Well, let me explain. I was in a quandary about subject matter as I sat down to write, and had searched through all my hunting and fishing stuff. Everything came up snake eyes, so I thought some more.

Ah, football would be a topic. But no, that's better in the hands of the competitive sportswriters. Besides, it's so overdone this time of year that the meat of the game is falling off the bones.

Well, I thought some more. Although, this winter we are about to be inundated with all manner of boat shows. Boats? Yes, boats. And looking at boating in more depth we find the subject matter is quite common to Michigan residents, as there are 900,000 members in the state's boating community. That's a large percent of the state's residents, and actually we lead the nation with registered watercraft. For a little trivia, there are nearly twice as many marinas in the state than there are McDonald's restaurants. Well, finally someone beat 'em!

So, looking at all this boating stuff finally triggered (pardon the expression) some ideas, including an experience of mine that didn't have boats as the primary focus, but none the less they were a factor.

So now, after all that flotsam and jetsam, let me tell you a little about a guy I'll always refer to as "Smitty the boat man."

"Smitty" was all we ever called him, although his name was Christopher Smith. He was one of my roommates during my first year of college. Smitty was likable, but not the gregarious type. Rather, he was an excellent student and spent much of his free time hitting the books.

He was a big-boned kid, well over six feet tall, but he suffered from both asthma and hay fever so wasn't out for football, basketball, or any other college sport. Rather, he always said that his big desire was to be around boats. At first, when he did talk, it was usually about sailing and the Navy, and his main drive in life was to be in the Navy and at sea, where he figured he could escape his allergies.

Well, Smitty eventually became a pal of mine, although our basic interests seemed different, and the two of us began to have fun by sneaking into several football games at Michigan State, along with crashing some fraternity parties that we were never invited to attend.

It never dawned on me at the time that Smitty would never have to sneak in to any event without paying. He wasn't a snappy dresser, and he owned a beat-up old Ford. However, he did have a rather fat wallet—that is, upon the times we got caught sneaking in at some event or when we needed some cash in a hurry.

I, on the other hand, was in college on a limited basketball scholarship, worked three evenings each week cleaning up in a Sears department store, and rarely had money for extracurricular activities. Neither did I go home on weekends as my home was several hundred miles distant, but Smitty jumped in his old Ford on many Friday evenings and took off for his home on Michigan's east coast somewhere.

But one Friday Smitty asked if I'd like to go to his home for the weekend. It was November and I hadn't been anywhere till then except around campus and eating dust at the old Sears store, so I took him up on the offer.

As we approached Smitty's home town, he asked, "I want to stop by the plant and see my dad a minute. Okay?" Of course I agreed.

We then skirted the town and proceeded along a road that led down to the water. Suddenly we were beside a large, sprawling factory with slips at the water's edge. And there I saw many beautiful, hand-crafted boats of all sizes rocking softly in the water.

Then I looked up and noticed a large sign over the factory—"Chris Craft." I looked over at Smitty in shear amazement. "You're that Smith?"

"Yea, I suppose so" was this "plain and simple" guy's reply!

33

Later, upon meeting and talking with Smitty's father, I came to understand why Smitty was the unassuming guy he was. He, like his father, was unpretentious and unerring, yet full of fun and even seemed like a devil-may-care individual ... but, sneaking into football games and crashing wild fraternity parties? Now you've got to be a down-to-earth guy to go along with that stuff!

Never again did I wonder or worry about Smitty, as we continued to wile away the off-hours of that first year at college by more "crashing" and "sneaking" and playing the old college games.

That spring I went off to the Korean War and Smitty drove off to I know not where. But I've since wondered if he was able to convince the Navy that his asthma and hay fever didn't matter. If so, perhaps he's enjoyed a life at sea. Or, perhaps he joined his father in the boat business.

I've not seen nor heard from Smitty since. But isn't it odd how we make good friends throughout our lives, tell them "goodbye and I'll see ya" one day, and never see them again? We continue to wonder perhaps, and then one day we realize that this life of ours doesn't come with an envelope full of instructions and directions, and that no man goes further than the one who really doesn't know where he's going, but goes ahead anyway ... perhaps "Smitty the boat man" is one of those who has gone far in this world. I hope so.

You may ponder all this if you like. Me? I'm preparing to attend a few boat shows—my old boat has had the course, and the empty trailer sits yawning at me in the back yard.

Butterfly Fishers Can Get into a 'Jam'

A favorite fishing spot of mine is on a tiny tributary that winds about like a snake and eventually intercepts the Grand River. At this particular juncture, the creek passes under a gravel roadway via a round, corrugated pipe.

Just through the entrance of that old pipe I've usually been able to hook into a nice brown trout, and this day, hot and in late summer when fish were scarce to nil, I decided to try my luck again. So I leaned over carefully to peer into the pipe.

As I looked I cradled a half-finished peanut butter and strawberry jam sandwich in one arm. Sure enough, several nice brownies lay in wait inside the passage.

I began to assemble my fly rod, and just then a large and beautiful Monarch butterfly flew up in front of me. It fluttered about in mid-air for a moment, then landed on my shirt near my left elbow. I shook my arm lightly and the butterfly flew off and down near the water, only to return to my elbow once more.

I was in wonderment at the beautiful creature's behavior until I looked closer to see what it was actually doing there—it was eating some of the strawberry jam that had accidentally rubbed onto my shirt from the sandwich.

I shook my arm lightly once more, and again the butterfly flew out and over the water, returning quickly to my arm and its jam lunch.

At that most opportune time a young fisherman wandered along the bank and hesitated. Then he inquired, "Did you ever catch anything under that old roadway?"

'Tis true that I will normally let a passing remark such as his go unrewarded, but it suddenly dawned on me that this was one of those scarce moments that just could not go by without an answer. My devilry rose up.

"Sure. Almost every time I've fished here," I replied. "That is, when I know there's a fish inside the pipe." I grinned, waiting for the boy to take the bait.

"Well, how do ya know there's any fish in there?" He'd taken it for sure.

"Here, I'll show you how," I answered with a grin while pointing to the butterfly on my arm. "Watch this."

I shook my arm again and the butterfly fluttered down toward the water, where he flew about a moment and returned to my arm.

"You mean you've got that there butterfly trained to spot fish?" queried the astonished youngster.

"Indeed I have. His name is Pete and good ol' Pete just informed me that there's a big one in there."

With that I lowered my poker-playing face and let an old bucktail fly drift down and into the pipe. There was a tremendous splash as a trout hammered the fly, and a moment later I had a 14-inch beauty upon the creek bank.

Now the kid was in total awe. "I don't believe it. Can he do it again?"

"Well now, let's just see," I smiled back, noting that good ol' Pete was again perched on my elbow. So I shook my arm once again, and once more the Monarch flew downward, fluttered over the water briefly, and returned to its jam.

"Yep," I sez, "Pete just told me there's another nice brown trout in there."

Once again I lowered the fly into the water, this time letting out more line to allow the bucktail to work its way deeper under the roadway.

Bang! Within a minute I had another large brownie up on the bank with the first one.

The youngster was absolutely beside himself by now.

"If I hadn't seen it with my own eyes, I'd never believe it," he stormed as he stomped about the area. "That's almost impossible!" Then, still muttering to no one in particular, he began to move slowly downstream. Then suddenly he hesitated and yelled through the brush, "By gosh, if you can do it then I can too ... I'm gonna catch me a butterfly and train 'em to spot fish for me."

"Well now, you can give it the old college try," I laughed back in his general direction, "but there's one thing I'd better warn you about. You've got to teach him not to get too close to the water when he's doin' his spotting. If he does, one of those big fellows is liable to rise up and get him ... You wouldn't want your butterfly to get into a jam like that, now would you?

I glanced at my arm then, and the butterfly was gone, its meal finished. But I was all smiles as I worked my way back to my truck ... butterfly fishing? Well, maybe not. But all in all, it had been a pretty good day.

Steelheading with the 'Hospital Boys'

Yes, I'm getting prepared for my wild turkey season to kick in, but steelhead fishing is almost at its peak and as I've said on numerous occasions, fishing is one of my favorite free-time items. Also, at this time of year, fishing seems to unclog the veins in even the most recluse or artery-frozen fisherman. Not that I'm a recluse, but I fish on a moment's notice.

And it was no exception that on a recent, cold morning I found myself out by the road at 4 a.m., thinking about how I'd gotten to bed at the 'cracker' dusk, arose before the 'cracker' dawn, and now would probably feel 'crummy' and cold the rest of the day.

However, there I was, fishing gear piled around me, awaiting four PA's from a local hospital to show up. We were heading over to the Pere Marquette River for a day of serious steelhead fly fishing. My pards would be Chuck, Jeff, Ben and Bill.

They finally arrived and we sandwiched ourselves into Chuck's club cab pickup. And, if you've ever tried fishing with six guys in a 10-foot rowboat you'll readily understand what that 86-mile trip in a jumpseat was like.

Well, sometime around 6 a.m. we uncoiled ourselves at the "high banks" that overlook the PM and strapped on our waders and other fishing gear, which included creature comforts such as warm gloves and coats. It was hovering around the freezing point and we knew ice would be on us as well as clogging up the furrows on our fly rods. We'd seen that before, so it wasn't really going to be a problem.

The first obstacle of the morning was to navigate about 200 steps that led down to the river, which I accomplished with little consequence except for imagining what the climb back up would be like.

Once at the river we spread out, upstream and downstream, as one thing you don't need while fly fishing is another guy getting your hook in his ear, or even having someone else scare the daylights out of a fish you've just spotted.

We were using orange and chartreuse yarn flies a we searched the riffles and bottom for gravel beds and runs where the fish would most likely be found hanging out.

Chuck tied into a big steelie almost immediately, but the hook wasn't set and the fish threw it with a few flashy moves as it tossed water some 15 feet in all directions.

I then caught a smaller one that surprisingly, and thankfully, didn't put on much of a show. The rule of the day was to 'catch and release,' and I couldn't help but imagine that fish in my smoker as I reluctantly gave it its freedom.

We fished on, and somewhat later Chuck and I crossed paths again, where he informed me that although it was slow going, he'd landed a nice rainbow and a brown trout. He'd also released them.

Eventually our group became further spread out, and after four hours of fishing I crawled up on the bank and sat on a log to rest my stream-pressured legs. Then along came Ben, one of the younger members of our party. He plopped himself down on the log too, and we chatted for a while about his days in the Army and mine in the Marines.

Then, as if to change the conversation, Ben remarked, "You know, around a hospital you hear all sorts of tales and woe, but since you like fishing I have one you'll probably appreciate." It seems that Ben was making his hospital rounds one morning, and in one of the beds lay a new patient with one leg up in traction and the other decorated with a heavily bandaged foot. Well, Ben asked the unlucky fellow how the injuries came about and was given the following account.

The man and a fishing partner had been after salmon on the Muskegon River, and fishing from their canoe. He said that a huge fish suddenly broke water right alongside them and landed smack dab in their canoe, and right by his partner's foot. Well now, his rocket scientist buddy, with a huge fish trying to get out of the canoe and not knowing what else to do, whipped out a Swiss Army knife and began to stab the fish.

Yup, you guessed it, he put that knife clean through his own foot!

Well, his partner had paddled like blazes for shore, all the while yelling for someone to call an ambulance or the paramedics. And someone did.

The upshot of the whole thing is that as they were toting the fellow up the steep hill on a stretcher, the guy was relating how the accident had come about. And the medic behind began laughing so hard that he dropped the tail end of the stretcher. Well, the hapless guy tumbled back down the bank, breaking the other foot in three places!

Now, did you get all this? Well, just like you, I took it right in, hook, line and sinker. That is, until that final punch, when I got a good laugh out of it.

"A true story!" I finally smirked. "I believe you stretched it a bit."

"Na," Ben grinned. "I did stretch it a little. But a good one, eh?"

"Time to go," said I. So we went our separate ways to fish on a while longer. Then we all met back at the steps, where we matched stories of our success, or the lack thereof.

As for the long climb back up to the truck? Well, all I can say is that the calves in both legs still ache. And that pretty much wrapped up our fishing day, except to say that after Ben's 'knife' story, the term 'steelheading' will always remind me of a Swiss Army knife and a day of fishing with the 'Hospital Boys.'

My Final Fly Fishing 'Presentation'

I once gave a neighbor a couple of fish, and he said they'd give his family a couple of great meals. Later the same month I gave him one of my old split bamboo fly rods, which he tried once before running out to buy an Orvis!

Guess you just can't please some people. But it was really my own fault, as I'd neglected to tell him that a fish doesn't give a hoot what you've paid for a fishing rod—or any other tackle for that matter.

Yes, a fish can be very particular about its food on any given moment. However, when fly fishing, a poor rod or even a poor fly imitation can catch fish. Presentation is the thing.

I know it's true, as I probably tie the worst imitations of anyone. But when presented to a fish in my half-fast way, my dumb flies will catch fish.

Sure, I own an Orvis, along with some other elite stuff. But believe it or not, I still prefer to cast with one of my old split bamboo fly rods. Yeah, they're heavier and can give one tennis elbow after three or four hours of whipping the waters to a froth, but their tip action is terrific.

And it's sometimes a real stitch to have other, nearby fishermen glance with disdain at me and my rod as they unkindly nudge this old "amateur" out of the way to pass by on a stream—they with their expensive outfits and me in my old hat, tattered clothes and ancient bamboo fly rod.

But once in a while I have the last laugh, as I follow behind 'em and snatch trout out of a stretch of river they've just fished.

And indeed such actually happened recently while fishing a stretch of the Pere Marquette River. After catching a few small trout almost out of his hip pocket, a guy with an expensive outfit waited for me to catch up.

"Hey, how are you doing that?" he asked, almost with a smirk. "I've got all this stuff that's supposedly guaranteed to catch 'em and I can't get a rise." With that he glanced down at my patched waders and up at my old fly rod. "You're catching 'em right in my wake."

I paused, returning the favor by eyeing his outfit and duds, then replied, "It isn't because I always use that expensive stuff. That gear usually remains locked up under the sportscap of my truck. I only get it out when the TV cameras are rolling." I gave a slight laugh, but he wasn't impressed as he glanced downward at his $900 fly rod and then back to my old bamboo (which is probably worth more than $900 to today's collectors—but I wasn't going to tell him that).

"Well," says he, apparently catching my drift, "Would you mind telling me your secret?"

"It's for certain this fly rod isn't any secret," I replied. "I use it sometimes because I really like the action. And I guess there are as many secrets to fly fishing as there are fish to the stream. But the only ones that really count, at least to me, are trying to match the hatch and fly presentation. Sometimes even an attractor fly works."

"They told me that stuff when I bought this equipment last week," he shot back. "All but the 'attractor' part. What's that?"

I thought I was really holding forth now, so continued, "Well, sometimes I can't match a hatch. That's when I go with a fly that's a bit flashy or entirely different—like the one I'm using now."

"You mentioned 'proper presentation,' he says. "Well, they gave me all of 10 minutes' instruction. You know. 10 'clock to 2 o'clock. Beyond that, I guess I'm not with it."

So I wiled away the next hour showing the guy some up-river, across-river and down-river techniques. Following that, he stood right there beside me and landed two trout!

Seeming well pleased, he finally remarked, "I certainly thank you for the advice." Then, extending a hand, he said, "My name's Joe Catchum. Nice meeting you, Ed. Now, I think I'll meander upstream some and further indoctrinate this here 'expensive' rod."

So Catchum went on fishing and I meandered back down-stream to the landing. And there, parked beside my truck, sat an expensive RV. And on its side, painted in bright red, were the words, "Catchum with Catchum's Tackle."

It was then obvious that I'd been had! And I thought as I read the sign, "I'll betcha if I chanced a peek inside this rig, I'd see two or more three-piece, split bamboo fly rods, a set of dilapidated fishing duds and a gigantic fly box with "Catchum" written all over it. Man, you've been had, but good, and I'll wager that old codger is laughing his fool head off right now...That was some "presentation" you made, wasn't it?"

Bait Too Big? Well, Maybe Not!

In all the world there is perhaps no better way to attract criticism or provoke unfavorable comment than to take a day off work and go fishing. Add to that simplicity a different or unordinary method of catching fish—such as angling for fish with another full-sized one as opposed to using a minnow—and you're a shoe-in for some sort of award. Even though you may catch tons of fish.

I'll regress and explain. I have this fishing buddy Ralph who has a little hideout on a small inland lake south of Mt. Pleasant. And one early morning ol' Ralphie jingles me to say he was going after some tackle-bustin' northern pike, and asked if my son Steve and I'd like to tag along to keep him honest.

Yeah, the answer affirmative, but I asked him what they'd be hitting on, thinking of spinners, spoons and other lures. He hurriedly informed me not to worry about all that hardware 'cause he already had all the bait we'd need.

"What kind of bait?" I asked.

"Got us some foot-long suckers," he says proudly.

Well, I'd known Ralph was somewhat of a ham since that time he told me another buddy of his had run off with his wife, but how he sorely missed his old buddy Joe. I decided to humor the rascal, called my son Steve, and off we went.

About an hour later the three of us clambered into Ralph's boat, and hazarding a glance into a noisy bucket, I discovered, certain as sin, about a dozen huge sucker minnows. "OK," I said. "Any leftovers I can toss into my smoker!"

Ralph shot me a hurt-like glance. "Wrong. Fact is, with this sort of fishing the bigger the bait the bigger the catch."

Steve and I gave him that old "I'm from Missouri" look, but he simply wound up the outboard and took us to a far corner of the lake. We anchored about 30 feet offshore and Ralph proceeded with the orders.

"Now, use one of the largest hooks in your tackle box and a medium weight slip sinker cuz you can keep the bait down in the water. Hook one of those suckers clean through both lips and just toss it overboard."

"So now what?" I snapped, as the huge suckers did everything but pull the anchor and drag us across the lake.

Ralph was unperturbed. "When a pike strikes the sucker, he'll usually hit it hard from the side and then run with it about 30 or 40 feet. So be ready to let him have all the slack line he wants. Just let him go, don't jerk on 'em, and eventually he'll stop for breakfast." He then ferreted a cookie from his cooler and began munching.

Steve suddenly let out a yelp. "Hey, something's nailed it!" His spinning rod was bent double and its tip rapidly disappeared under the boat when Ralph calmly reached over and opened the bail on the reel.

"There," Ralph says with the coolness of a head of lettuce. "You got one looking for a full course. Just let him have all the hors d'oeuvres he wants."

Ralph and I reeled in our lines and I hauled up the anchor while Steve got anxious. "Can I hit him now?" he asked nervously.

"Here now," says Ralph, "just get yourself a sandwich and a coke from the cooler and relax. He's gnashing his choppers on that sucker right now, but soon he'll turn it around so it's head-first and swallow it. Then you can take up slack line until you feel him and give it a good yank. I'll tell you, there's nothing quite as furious as a northern when you've hooked it deep."

So there Steve sat, with a mythical monster on line as he sat sampling a ham and cheese sandwich. Ralph and I sat there too, each sipping coffee.

Following an eternity of about six minutes, ol' Ralph looked up and said quietly, "Now."

Steve reeled in slack line and then remarked something to the effect that "something was doggone heavy out there." Then he whipped back on the spinning rod.

Well, it wasn't a mythical monster, nor the bottom of the lake. It moved too fast for that. The huge northern busted water right off our bow, twisting as it leaped. The mangled sucker flew through the air like a silver bullet, smacking yours truly right across the nose! But the hook was firmly imbedded and Steve had on a beauty.

The next 20 minutes proved a tug and run contest, and the pike didn't push another nostril above the surface until it was tamed. Finally, I reached behind its head and lifted the fish into the boat.

Following that excitement, Ralph caught a beauty. Steve became completely obnoxious and I got whitewashed. But Steve's fish made the day as later it would tip the scale at 16 pounds and almost make a yardstick disappear.

But our day was not yet completely made. That afternoon we sat eating a couple of belly-bomb burgers when we overheard a couple of fellow anglers yakking in a nearby booth. "I saw the dangdest thing out on the lake today," one of them said. "Three suckers sitting out there and fishing with huge suckers. Never saw such idiots! There ain't no whales in that lake."

Well now, two converts looked over at their mentor a moment, let out a couple of silly grins, and thought about that huge "sucker" northern on ice out in their truck!

The motor came off the transom…

Not Just Another 'Fish Story'

It was nearing midnight and I'd been fishing for several hours on a stretch of river about a half mile below a small dam. Not having much success on this, one of my favorite areas and noted mostly for German brown trout, I'd finally given up and was hiking along a dark path back upstream toward my truck when I heard a sharp noise up ahead.

The noise wasn't like the snapping of a tree branch but quite similar to the springing of a trap.

Stopping, I turned off the small headlamp on my cap, wondering what my next move should be. Then the springing "whump" came again, followed by splashing water and an excited voice saying, "I got the bugger!"

So someone was definitely in the stream up ahead. I moved slowly through the darkness, and was finally able to see two men in the middle of the stream, one brandishing a flashlight and the other a small spear gun.

The guy with the light also had a sack over a shoulder, presumably with fish in it.

I moved onward a few steps as the pair made their way on up the gravel-bottomed stream, and suddenly bumped into something—not a tree, but another individual!

"Quiet!" came a low but authoritative voice. "I'm a conservation officer and I've been watching these clowns for some time now. When they get up closer to the dam I'll arrest 'em."

Then there was a moment of hesitation, and flipping a small penlight in my face he asked quickly, "You're not with them, are you?"

"No," I whispered. "I've been fishing downstream. I've no idea who they are and didn't know what they were up to until a moment ago… looks like they're spearing trout."

"Sure are, and they've several in that sack already…You sure you're not with them?" he repeated.

"No, I don't know who they are and the only thing I've ever speared is suckers up in—."

"There, they just got another one," he interrupted. "Looks like the school will be having fish for lunch tomorrow."

"School? What school?"

"Well, sometimes I keep a fish or two for myself when I catch violators," he whispered, but most times I take 'em to the cooks at the local school. The kids love 'em."

So I followed the CO's steps along the path for about another half hour, during which the pair in the river speared several more fish.

Suddenly the dam, which had a pole light above it, came into view. Then the CO moved swiftly ahead, approaching the men and making the arrest as they exited the stream.

I remained in the background as the officer counted out the fish, put them back in the sack and placed it in his vehicle, and then ordered the men inside as well. Then they sped off, presumably for the local lock-up. I walked over to the spot where the arrest was made and the fish counted, and there on the ground was about a four-pound German brown trout.

Had the officer merely forgotten the fish? Well, I figured that wasn't the case. Instead, he'd probably left it for me, so I scooped it up and put it on ice in my Ranger.

Upon arriving home that late evening I told my wife what had happened. "Well now," she scoffed, saying, "Never happened! You caught this beauty yourself, didn't you?…Good story, though!"

I guess she ignored the spear holes in the fish, but I can tell you that it did actually happen that way. And maybe it just goes to prove that wives all think their fisherman husbands are liars…Maybe even more so when they actually bring home a fish!

Canoe Flying Downriver

I recently grabbed at the opportunity to again go "canoe-flying" down the river with an old fishing buddy. Actually, I was cleaning up some fly-fishing gear and preparing to put it away when good ol' John called.

"Hey, there's some fish coming up into the stretch," he said excitedly. "Let's go do it! We can spot your rig down below and put my canoe in at M-37…How about Saturday?"

He needn't have said all that, as I was ready when I first heard his voice and we both knew the routine. We'd done it almost every summer for several years.

We'd spot my truck downstream at Bowman Bridge, on the Pere Marquette River about seven miles west of Baldwin, then haul his rig with the canoe upstream of the M-37 bridge, a couple miles south of Baldwin. There we'd put in to fish. The trip downstream and the manner in which we'd fly fish would occupy the better part of a day.

The word here is, if you fishermen out there want a day of fishing combined with challenge and excitement and haven't tried canoe "flying" down a river, you're missing out on a great experience. And of course, you don't need the Pere Marquette (PM) River to do it—try it on any favorite stream, preferably one with a run of hungry fish.

There are certain items you should be aware of prior to putting in at the river. Some are fun, while others may be hazardous to your health.

The first concerns deal with the hazardous side. First, it takes two in the canoe, no more and no less, to take the trip; one in front to be fishing while the person aft handles the paddle. One person can't really do both, and a third party in the middle can most certainly be in harm's way. The other hazard could become reality if you don't choose a good fishing partner. That is, you must be certain that he, or she, is fairly proficient at flipping flies—that they at least be capable of making an upward or a correct sideward cast and retrieve. If they are not, you could find yourself with a fly embedded in an ear or some other uncomfortable part of your anatomy! Ouch!

That's two, but I may as well mention another hazard while on the subject—a little item known as "sweepers." Those are much as the name implies, trees overhanging or sometimes actually in the water, bent over from bank erosion around their roots. These, if not avoided, can sweep your canoe around, over, or sometimes under, and can pin people under the water as well.

Ah, but forgetting the above pitfalls for the moment, let's dwell on the more pleasant parts of such a venture.

You push off downstream, letting your buddy do the fishing first, of course. You work the river slowly, controlling the canoe and keeping an eye out for the best path or run to follow.

Occasionally one of you may spot a likely fishing hole ahead, and this gives you some choices. You can beach the canoe and both fish awhile, or you can let out the small anchor (the one you almost forgot to bring along) and "drag" slowly through the area, allowing time for both to cast some flies.

Fishing gear depends not only upon the weather but upon all conditions. Frankly, John and I go as light as possible, taking only one fly rod each and storing our fly cases and other extras in our fishing vests. We found it best not to burden ourselves with tackle boxes and other paraphernalia that just won't be used. Of course, a sandwich and beverage or two can come in handy.

If you do go "flying" down a river in this manner you'll most certainly enjoy it. And perhaps more on a second or third trip, as you'll have discovered certain runs or holes where the steelhead, salmon and other fish hang their hats or lay in a holding pattern on their way upstream.

Oh, I'd better fill you in on this trip. Well, about two hours downstream we hit one of our favorite spots, with a long stretch of gravel in the middle and a deep run along the left bank. At that point we beached the canoe and both fished. Each landed a steelhead there, plus John was fortunate enough (or expert enough) to haul in several dandy brown trout during the remainder of our journey.

We hadn't picked a high-water day and encountered no dangerous sweepers during the voyage. All said, it was a great day of "flying" the river. Try it sometime if you haven't already done so. And if you have, maybe you can give John and me some pointers. Yeah, I know, they say you can't teach an old dog new tricks, but these "old dogs" will at least listen.

A Few Spring and
Summer Fishing Stories

I'm in the mood for a few stories about spring and summer fishing.
A few of the following were gleaned from a "Boats & Notes"
publication, while others are a figment of perhaps my own
imagination. At any rate, I believe you may enjoy them.

Here goes...

*It seems a conservation officer stopped a man who was carrying
two buckets of fish. So he asked the fellow, "Do you have a license to
catch those fish?"

The man replied, "No, sir, I don't need a license. These are my pet
fish."

"Pet fish?" the astonished officer asked.

"Yes, sir," the fisherman replied. "Every night I take these here
fish down to the lake so they can swim around for a while. Then I
whistle, and they jump back into their buckets. Then I taken 'em back
home."

"Now, that's crazy! Fish can't do that!" replied the officer.

The guy looked at the officer a few moments and then said, "It's not
crazy. I'll show you."

"O.K.," said the officer. "Do it now!"

So the fisherman quickly poured the fish into the lake and stood
waiting. After several minutes, the officer turned to the man and asked,
"Well?"

"Well, what?" the fisherman responded.

"Well, when are you going to call 'em back?" the officer asked.

"Call who or what back?" the man asked.

"The FISH!" yelled the officer.

"Now, what fish?" asked the fisherman.

*Real boaters consider a bucket of chicken or a peanut butter & Jelly sandwich to be perfectly acceptable to serve guests. They also know how to change their own oil—don't always do it, but they know how. They have often called in sick to go boating and showed up to work the next morning with a tan. They also wear clothes that are comfortable, no matter how they look to anyone else. They can fix anything with duct tape, but within a week will no longer notice it. They will also seethe with anger when invited to a wedding or a children's party on a Saturday in the summer. And real boaters own the saying, "It's only a little shower. Ignore those clouds and lightning over there!"

*A boater became shipwrecked. When he awoke, he found himself on a beach with dark red sand. He can hardly believe it as he looks around. The sky is dark red, and on the ground is dark red grass. He also sees dark red birds and dark red fruit growing on dark red trees. Then, he's really shocked when he discovers that his skin is starting to turn dark red.

"Oh no!" he cries out. "I believe I've been marooned!

*It seems that a herd of buffalo can only move as fast as the slowest one in the bunch, not unlike the brain, which can only operate as fast as the slowest brain cells. The slowest buffalo are usually sick or weak, so they die off first. And such makes it possible for the herd to move at a faster pace. And like the buffalo, the weak or slow brain cells are the ones killed off by excessive drinking of pop and excessive fishing, which makes the brain operate at a faster pace…So, the moral of the story is, if you drink more pop and fish more it will make you smarter!

You know, there is an old Chinese proverb that says, "There are people who really fish, and then there are those that simply disturb the water." Having fished all my life, I'm still uncertain as to which applies to me. However, I've always thought it wasn't just the catchin' but the fishin' that really mattered. After all, as that famous bard once said, "The play's the thing!"

Weird Willie's Secret Tackle Box

True to my usual pursuits, I fished for bass and landed a trout. Can't imagine how or why I manage to do such things—seems I've nearly always set out to do one thing and accomplished another.

Anyway, a rather uncouth and sometimes fishing buddy—let's just call him weird Willie to protect the poor fellow—and I decided to try our skill one recent morning on the Flat River.

Now Willie is fun to fish alongside, but he isn't exactly what one could call a scientific angler. Fact is, the bass tackle he brought along that morning consisted of a short, stiff old spinning rod with what appeared to be 50-pound test line and a reel that he worked upside down and backwards. Oh, and he toted a cigar box held together with a large rubber band—called it his "secret" tackle box.

When Willie wasn't looking I took a sneak peek into that box, and there didn't seem to be much ado about his big secret. It contained a half-eaten sandwich, an old Jitterbug lure that must have belonged to his grandfather, and a tangled collection of spinners and treble hooks along with some bell sinkers that were so huge and heavy they seemed destined to k.o. a fish on the way down.

However weird all this may seem and just in case you haven't guessed, Willie is what you'd call a sleeper—always acts as though he's wondering about the greater mysteries of life, such as why doesn't Bill Bailey ever come home, when all the while he actually knows what he's doing ... Sometimes I can hate a guy like that!

So that early morning we motored to a spot on the river where another real bass fisherman and I'd caught bass before. It was up and alongside some reeds and lily pads.

"Hey now, move right up in there," Willie directed, pointing toward the middle of the tangle of lily pads. "That's where the bigger fish are."

"Now hold on," says I, "just who invited who along on this fishing trip?"

"Well," smirked Willie, "the bass ain't out here right now, they're in under them lily pads."

Somehow I was suddenly reminded of what my old high school football coach once secretly told me when our team was down 35-0 at halftime: "You can handle any adversity if you think you can. Just keep a cool head and a sense of humor." (Well, I'd done that, and only lost 54-0!)

In a way, that helped me to humor Willie. I cut the outboard, grabbed the oars, and pulled the boat into the center of those lily pads. Willie was looking like a kid in a sweet shop with money burning a hole in his pocket. Never said a word, just beamed and looked to his secret box.

So, figuring I'd never get indigestion from eating my own words, I assembled my fly rod and pawed around in my vest for some poppers, while informing the character that all was just fine. I could still reach out into the main stream with my fly line, and he was welcome to fish for them frogs!

Then I made a few casts, all the while keeping an eye on my weird partner. And what he did seemed almost disgusting. First, he put a gigantic spinner on his line, attached there by a swivel about the size of a diaper pin. Then he tied granny knots to attach a huge bell sinker about six inches above the spinner. "There now," he says, tooting a wicked grin, "that auta hold 'em!"

I momentarily neglected my own fishing and watched as he reached out with that stiff rod and dropped the lure into a small space among the pads. Then he began to slowly work the rod tip up and down. Suddenly the tip stopped dancing, and within three seconds Willie had horsed up about a four-pound bass. Hard to believe, but there it was, flopping around in the bottom of the boat!

It was then that I realized I needed to quell my previous thoughts about Willie and his weird methods. "Hey, that's great—how can I rig my fly rod to do that?"

"Can't. Not with that rod and light line," he replies, as he repeats the same feat on the opposite side of the boat—a smaller bass this time, but not by much.

"You need a heavy rod and heavy line 'cause you gotta horse 'em up. Otherwise they'll tangle you up in the pads an' weeds an' you'll lose 'em. Got to get 'em up quick."

Well now, weird Willie was suddenly not so weird anymore. Instead, he'd now become one of the wisest fishing pals I've yet to know—secret cigar box and the whole nine yards! So I rather half-heartedly turned about and began flipping a popper into the deeper water, while sort of wishing I'd brought along my old Ugly Stick rod and some rope-sized line—and maybe even a secret cigar box of my own.

Several hours later we put an end to it. Willie with his limit of some of the nicest bass you'd ever want to catch, and me with one lowly German brown trout.

But as I said, it seems as though things like this invariably happen to me ... You know, using the elite, expensive tackle rather than the stuff that actually works, or catching the species of fish I'm not actually fishing for, etc....Yeah, I really do hate it when that happens.

Gone Fishin'—at the Class Reunion

The wife and I trekked north recently to do a little scouting and fishing. And, as a lark, to attend a class reunion. It was that time of year for those reunions, and somehow you feel obligated to show up.

So, after fishing that afternoon, we went to the affair in our old fishing duds. There I began to 'fish' about for someone I actually could recognize. It was amazing how everyone was now somewhat older than me. Some were dressed up in their fit-to-kill suits or fancy dresses, while I wore my smelly fishing clothes and sported a stubble of beard along with a moustache.

Gratefully, I wasn't easily recognized either! But someone did.

A former classmate finally bellied up to our table as though he too were fishing for someone he knew, and asked hesitantly, "You're Ed, right?"

I nodded that I was the guilty party and he stuck out a hand as he continued, "Remember me? I'm Don, the guy who never had any money. But I arrived in a stretch limo this time, just to put on the dog. Actually, I'm broke, as usual...But hey, why the salt-and-pepper beard and moustache?"

I'd noticed that as he questioned me he'd been taking in my ragged fishing clothes, so decided to play his game.

"Well Don, " I said straight-faced, 'the wife and I've been out on the river fishing. And actually, I'm getting prepped to play the lead in Hemingway's 'The Old Man and the Sea.' This is part of my makeup."

"You mean you're going to play that lead on stage? Wow, that's great!"

"Actually, I'm not," I told him. "I'll be playing the lead shark."

"All right!" he snorted, his eyeballs rolling up at the ceiling. Then he scurried off to scout for some other poor fish.

Then, as I polished off a Coke and prepared to enjoy dinner, another classmate came fishing. Following the niceties, she pointed to another table and whispered, "That's Helen over there. You'd better say hello to her and act as though you remember her or she's going to feel awful."

"Helen? Helen who?" I asked, peering at the strange woman with the wrinkled face.

"You remember her, I'm sure. Goodness, you two were an item back in school. The problem is that after high school she married a guy from way down south and soaked up too much sun down there. You know what that can do to someone."

So I thanked her, whoever she was, and ambled over to that other total stranger. We pretended it was old home week for a few minutes and the lady was all smiles when I retreated. I still don't believe I've ever seen her before, but as I returned to my table I was thinking that everyone should occasionally pick out a stranger in the crowd and do likewise—that it may become a kinder, gentler world if everyone did.

So I 'fished' about the gathering some more, and it seemed amazing how the homely-lookers back in high school were suddenly much prettier, while the formerly good-lookers had changed considerably for the worst.

Case in point, a girl named Nancy who'd been somewhat of a homely one years ago and had tried to snare me all through high school, was now beautiful and belle of the ball! I started to get up to go over and introduce myself, but an unusual look in my wife's eyes quickly thwarted that idea. I guess I correctly theorized that some things are better left undone.

But the real surprise of the evening was that the kid who'd probably been the worst cut-up in our class was not only the MC for the affair but was now a college professor. I tried to reckon with that one and concluded he'd somehow just got smarter.

I fished about some more, and two men were present that I easily recognized. They were brothers, Tom and Jack, boys I'd grown up with. They'd been constant fishing, hunting, and camping companions during our youth. We shared some memories and are going to make some more as we're going to fish together again this fall.

Of course some of my best friends didn't show up at the reunion, and five of those will not be around in the future. And such brings to mind the last stanza of a poem a classmate once penned:

"Whatever the reason friends aren't here, in thoughts we'll shed a lonely tear. We'll pause a moment to recall, the empty chairs within this hall."

My take on that? Well, those chairs may be empty but I'm quite certain those friends are still around … they've just gone fishing.

Fishing vs. Yard Sales:
The Battle Continues

It seems as though I fight this same battle each summer while en route to or from a fishing trip up north. But somehow, it only heats up when I take my wife along.

It's the "fishing vs. yard sale" battle. Sure, we're gliding along past all those beautiful lakes and rivers we could be fishing, but those never seem to be on her itinerary. Nope, it's those yard sale signs she sees.

"There's one! Oh, look, there's another! Let's stop here a minute." And the battle is on once more.

Now, I always prepare meticulously for most fishing trips, which I usually take alone or with another fisherman. But this one wouldn't be an extended trip, just a day, so I thought I'd ask my wife Gerri to accompany me. Of course she was delighted at the very idea—not for the fishing, mind you, but about the prospect of bouncing through all those yard sales along the way.

Sure, I was a little concerned at first, almost knowing what I'd be in for, but perhaps it would be a gracious idea. She'd perhaps tie into a nice trout or two, and maybe not bother me about stopping so many times. After all, a doctor friend once told me that taking my wife fishing could actually add years to my life...Yes, it certainly has. I feel at least 20 years older now!

"Look at that sale! It's huge!" she suddenly pointed out.

Her remark broke my melancholy, and thinking it may be merely a passing fancy, I decided to humor her. So I pulled the Ranger over and she bailed out to go bouncing through row upon row of old furniture, mowers, pots and pans, and other smashed or broken-down treasures. Finally, she grabbed up several old, chipped dishes and a few cups, saying these would come in handy when we have company.

"We're going to offer guests old stuff like this?" I asked glancing at the pitiful things.

"I can repair them," was all she replied. And that was that.

Realizing that living with a saint can often be as grueling as trying to be one, I paid up and stashed the stuff in the back of the truck, taking care not to whack any of the fishing gear but secretly hoping the gear would whack the dishes. No such luck.

She let me bypass the next sale. It was an auction, and I told her it was where one could get 'something' for 'nodding'." No, she didn't catch the joke, but I wasn't catching any fish either.

Well, two more sales loaded up the Ranger with clothing, kid's dolls and numerous other items which no doubt will be displayed at our next garage sale.

Ah, but we were finally at our destination, alongside the North Branch of the Pere Marquette River. There, I rigged up a "pole" for her and my own fly rod, and escorted the wannabe fisherlady to a likely looking spot on the stream. I left her there and proceeded downstream.

Suddenly, "I have one, I think!" floated down to me, and I hurried to her side to find about a 12-inch rainbow trout flopping at her feet.

"Hey! Nice fish!" I said. "Wanna keep it?"

Her answer being unpublishable, I'll just say that I cleaned it and stashed it in our ice chest for posterity. After all, I figured it would be the only one she'd catch.

Well, as usual, I was wrong. After that, she landed an 11-inch brookie. I, on the other hand, the great fisherman, landed but one keeper.

"I'm starving," I finally remarked. "Let's tool into town and get a fish sandwich or something."

So off we went to eat—and to make one more yard sale on the return trip.

And now, as I write, I'm reminded of a stop a couple years ago, when Gerri purchased a giant replica of an owl. It now perches on a branch of a pine tree alongside our patio. And it seems to be glaring back at me, asking "Whooo? Whooo's the better fisherman now?"

It seems that piece of plastic asks the same question whenever I look up at it. But I know in my heart that owls can't really talk, although some say they can. And if an owl ever talks to you, tell it to shut up. After all, it's really lying!

Two Deaf-Mutes on the River

I was flipping flies at steelhead that lay in the waters of the Pere Marquette River on a recent outing and either the fish could care less, were just plain lazy or were having a bad fin day.

Each time a fish rose he merely nudged the fly or really didn't inhale it.

Perhaps I was just a little too quick on the trigger.

The truth is that rather than letting a fish smash the fly, I was over-anxiously whipping up the rod tip and jerking the fly from the fish's mouth.

I know better than to do that, but I didn't immediately recognize my mistake.

Someone else did.

Another fisherman had slowly edged his way upstream toward me. When I finally took notice of him, he was staring at me like I had the brains of a lump of coal. Then he suddenly began to gesture with his hands and the tip of his own fly rod.

I thought he must be a deaf-mute, could neither hear nor talk and must be using some sort of sign language. It was obvious because he'd flip a fly out on the water and then pretend to get a fish strike.

Then he'd wait a second or so before whipping the rod back, grinning as though he'd tied into a big one.

So I nodded and grinned back at the poor fellow while raising my rod tip slowly several times.

He smiled back, not uttering a sound.

It suddenly dawned on me that he believed two deaf-mutes had mysteriously met on the same river. He believed I couldn't hear or speak either.

The two of us fished on in fairly close proximity for a while. Suddenly he had a good-sized steelhead on line. So I worked my way through the water to the bank and to a position below him, finally netting his fish for him.

The lucky fellow came toward me then, gesturing, smiling and pointing to the fish, about a six-pounder, as though he'd already grilled it and was eating it at a table.

I bowed gracefully in his direction and he did likewise.

Then I moved on upstream a ways as he continued to fish somewhat below me.

Then it happened. A huge steelhead smashed at my streamer fly and once again I struck too soon, taking the fly right from the fish's mouth. No, not again, I thought.

I glanced over at the fellow again. This time he was really excited. He was using some sort of sign language, trying to tell me with some obvious anger that once again I was not letting a fish take the hook.

This time I gestured at him with a free hand, trying to indicate that I not only understood, but wouldn't let such an awful thing happen again.

But it did, you see. I made one more lazy cast and when a dandy German brown trout suddenly rose to the fly, I once again whipped the rod tip upward. I could see the fly lodged in the corner of the fish's mouth but it took a sudden sideways flip and flash—the fly came loose again.

Then I heard a string of words—expletives deleted—and looked to see the guy exiting the water and glaring back at me.

Then he hollered back at me, "By all the fishing Gods, I have never seen such a stupid deaf-mute.

"You will never learn to be a trout fisherman if you live to be a hundred and only fish in stocked fish ponds.

"What a dummy you are."

So it turned out that neither of us was actually deaf or mute, simply a couple of frustrated steelhead fishermen.

And the very poor fellow had been merely trying to correct me when I erred.

Totally confused by the incident, I stood there thinking that maybe I should just leave trout fishing to the experts and stick to hunting. Or maybe, just maybe I should move to Bolivia or somewhere and get a job driving a truck.

A Life-Threatening Experience
on the Big Lake

The day began innocently enough. Several of us were sitting around the table at our early-morning coffee hour at one of the local coffee joints. We had cussed and discussed everything from politics to salmon, and I was about to get on with the day when suddenly one of the old-times, Freeman (Freem to us) turned to me.

"My son has a Sea Ray in a slip over at the marina on Muskegon Lake," Freem remarked. "How about I give him a call? It's a beautiful day. We could meet him in North Muskegon and the three of us go out for some salmon."

The offer was too much to refuse. An hour later I met Freem at the marina, where he informed me that he'd been unable to contact his son. But he assured me that he knew the boat from "A to Z" so we could still make the trip.

Now I must tell you that Freem was then 81 years of age and not quite as agile as in his younger days. His real love had been fly fishing in streams, but he'd given that up some years earlier due to a weakness in his legs.

The lake was calm, so Freem took the craft out of the slip, over Muskegon Lake and through the channel into Lake Michigan. The boat was a 27-foot Sea Ray with twin 260 MerCruisers, and a beautiful piece of equipment.

As we exited the channel, I saw fish blipping on his fishfinder, and mentioned that it might be a good idea to try it right there. His answer was in the negative, claiming the old fishfinder must be incorrect as the real fish had to be about two miles out. I wasn't insistent about giving the mouth of the channel a try, so we continued on.

After a smooth ride, we arrived at his spot, about two miles from shore. Several fish were appearing on the finder at about an 80-foot depth, so we set the downriggers and Freem cut it to trolling speed.

Within half an hour we'd made several passes about the area without any success. Meanwhile, Coast Guard warnings were coming in and I was keeping an ear to the radio plus an eye to the west.

Then I saw it. There was a very dark front along the horizon, and stretching north to south as far as the eye could see. I motioned to Freem and pointed to the line of clouds which seemed to be getting closer by the moment.

"They're a long ways off," Freem scoffed. "We have time for another pass or two over the area.

I was skeptical, but answered with a hesitant nod and we came about for another run. About fifteen minutes later the wind had picked up considerably, chopping at the Sea Ray, and I told Freem (now, insisted was more like it) that we'd better get our tails off the lake.

This time he agreed, and we reeled in the lines and headed for the harbor. But by the time we were within a half-mile of shore the full force of the wind and rain hit us, knocking the boat about like a cork and forcing us to hold fast.

Then something happened that I'd never witnessed before, haven't since, and that I've indeed not told many about until now. Suddenly Freem backed away from the wheel and retreated to a seat at the transom where he simply sat down and stared straight ahead, not saying a word.

He'd left the boat completely on its own, and it was heading erratically toward shore slightly north of the channel.

I'd watch him manipulate the craft while on the way out and during our fishing runs, but never had I operated one this size and so equipped.

I yelled at Freem, but he continued to stare straight ahead and made no reply.

We were rapidly approaching shore now, and the huge swells were beating at us when I finally grabbed the wheel. My first thought was to beach the Sea Ray, and then it struck me that were I to do that, the boat would be wrecked and there was a good chance that neither of us would reach shore alive.

I kicked it hard to port and went back out, circling about to make a run at the channel. Then I saw the huge swells rolling into the channel mouth and pounding over the south seawall. We were coming in too close to that wall, and that was undoubtedly where we'd end up. I came about again, went to the north and this time brought it along the north wall. But the huge waves and swells lifted and drove us again and again toward the south wall. Then, as we came within what must have been but a foot from the wall, the Sea Ray came about and grudgingly into the channel. Within a minute or so we were into calmer water, and then into Muskegon Lake.

Then an even more amazing thing occurred.

Suddenly Freem was standing beside me, took control, and said calmly, as though nothing had happened, "I've got it." Whereupon he took the boat cross the lake and calmly backed it into its slip at the marina.

We spoke nothing of the incident at the time, and did not ever after. Freem has since gone to where I believe all true fishermen go, and my hope is that he is out there festooning his fly line in some trees over one of his favorite trout streams, with young and strong legs once again.

Writer's note: This incident actually happened to me several years ago. For a long time I put it out of my mind and refused to talk or write about it. But perhaps it is best told, and can be taken as a lesson for anyone fishing the Big Lake.

Old Photo Brings on Memories

I'm looking at an old photo of my father that hangs on the wall over my desk, and old but warm memories are flooding to mind.

My father, Donald Gilbert, gone some years past, is still considered the epitome of the outdoor individual by me. A hero, in fact. And we all have heroes. He was mine.

My dad carried a steel plate in his left shoulder where a German machine gunner had blown part of it away over in France during World War I. But he overcame the disability to work, hunt and fish with the best of men. And to be my mentor as well.

Dad began his outdoor career back in the 1930's, when we lived in the little town of Alanson, just north of Petoskey. He worked for the Conservation Department at the Oden Fish Hatchery, but his opportunity came when he earned the chance to attend Conservation School at Higgins Lake.

Upon graduating from the school, he picked us up—lock, stock and barrel —and relocated the family to Baldwin. There, he became manager of the Department's Baldwin Trout Rearing Station. It was 1942, I was a youngster and World War II was raging away in far-flung places.

I recall that at first it was a scary move for me—from the old house in Alanson to a much newer and larger home. A home that was surrounded by 18 trout ponds and a river flowing between them, with several back-waters and unknown forests standing throughout the area.

Dad became very busy immediately. He had three employees to handle and about 400,000 brook, rainbow and brown trout to raise. But he found time in the evening hours for fishing, and we began to enjoy that together. It was a pastime that eventually must have led us to all 156 lakes and 47 trout streams within Lake County.

He wasn't much for fly fishing, but did use a fly rod and a long leader tipped with bait. He was good at fishing, and gradually indoctrinated me into the love of fishing. I thank him for that. Yes, we also hunted together, and he was an expert with either a shotgun or the old, war-surplus 30.06 he owned. I recall tagging along on a particular deer hunt when he shot a huge 8-point buck through the neck at about 400 yards—without a scope!

A few years later I was allowed to carry a gun and to hunt alongside him. And one of the first things I learned was to identify my target. We were after snowshoe rabbits in the Baldwin/Luther swamp, when I saw some movement in the brush and fired at it. Dad asked me if I'd seen exactly what had moved before firing, and upon admitting that I hadn't, I suddenly found myself flat on my back from a blow to the chest. Cruel? No, it was a lesson learned and one I'll never forget.

My father was a multi-faceted individual, and often involved in activities beyond his fish ponds or hunting and fishing. He called for square dances at the old village gym, and was also a loyal member of the township fire department. He was particularly loyal when the members of the fire department gathered for their weekly poker night.

Well, the years came and went, and dad retired when I was overseas with the Marines. And he never seemed quite the same in later years— read a lot and sat about much of the time…Still, we occasionally hunted and fished together.

Yes, I recall those many enjoyable times as I look up at the photo of him standing on the old iron bridge over the Baldwin River—rod in hand, old cloth creel dangling at his side, and a smile, always a smile, on his face.

An Ice Fishing Memory

S itting on a wooden crate on the ice at Murray Lake while trying to pull up a mess of bluegill and crappies was the hardest part of a recent ice fishing trip. So was weathering the northwest breeze that held the wind-chill below zero.

The easy part was staring at the tip of my ultra-light rig, waiting for it to dance, and becoming mesmerized. But occasionally the tip of the rod would quiver and I'd winch up a "slabber" or a gill. Still, that wasn't the real enjoyment.

The interesting thing was that sitting there brought back the memory of a long ago ice fishing excursion. What it had been was a two-day winter campout along Cashion Lake up in Lake County, with two of my chums, Jack and Tom McLenithan. It was a planned campout, and we took along only the necessities—a pup tent with no bottom, a few cook pots and a fry pan, bed rolls and of course an ax to chop through the ice and our fishing gears.

Ulta-light rods and power augers didn't really exist in those days, just an ax and the little stick rods with the standard black line. But two tip-ups for pike fishing were in our arsenal, although we had no idea what we'd use for bait once the minnows were discovered frozen to death on our 2-mile hike to the lake.

Jack, two years the senior of Tom and me, proved to be more resourceful than we 11-year-olds—he packed along a .22 rifle and a pocket of ammo, saying it was just in case the fishing was lousy. If so, he'd bump off a rabbit or squirrel to eat.

After trudging through more than a foot of snow and with more coming down, we arrived lakeside and set up camp under a grove of snow-laden fir trees. We first scraped an area clear of snow and set up the pup tent, then cut some branches off the trees and placed them on the ground, tossing our bed rolls over them. Then we built a large fire in front of the tent.

Off to the fishing, I, proclaiming myself as the expert at cutting fishing holes, managed to chop through about 8 inches of ice before handing the ax to Jack. Then I hooked a dead minnow to my tip-up and lowered it through one of the holes. Tom fished the other hole, also with a minnow, while Jack made a larger hole and then proceeded to cut a minnow into little chunks, which was bait for his small rod.

Well, Tom and I watched as Jack hauled up one gill after another, all the time informing us that we'd better use minnow pieces if we wanted to catch anything but colds.

Suddenly the flag on my tip-up flew upward and I grabbed the line. And soon I had a large fish flopping on the ice. A monster bass! But bass weren't in season. And I was about to put the fish back into the hole when Jack told me to place it in the fish bucket along with his gills—that nobody would be the wiser. Besides, the bass would make a fine supper. So I did as I was told.

Within a couple of hours we had enough fish in the bucket and on the ice to feed thrashers, if there'd been any around, so we called it quits and returned to camp. There we discovered that our large fire, left to its own devices, had warmed the overhead branches and had not only splashed out the fire, but had collapsed our tent under several feet of snow.

Later on, after cleaning up the mess and building a new, even larger pitch-pine fire, we started frying the fish.

It was then that Duffy, a local conservation officer, arrived on the scene. He'd seen the smoke and came to investigate. He greeted us and then stared suspiciously at the large fish in our frying pan. Then he told us with a wry grin that it was the largest bluegill he'd ever seen, wished us well and walked off. We all vowed that henceforth he'd be a friend of ours.

Early the next morning, Jack woke us up and told us to follow him. So, we grudgingly put on our boots and he led us to a spot about 100 yards from camp, where he told us to look up in a nearby tree. We did, and there sat four grouse.

Jack raised his .22 and fired, and the lower of the pats fell dead to the ground. The remaining birds didn't move, so one by one he felled all four, always shooting the lowest to the ground. Tom and I were awestruck!

Then a thought suddenly occurred to me, so I tugged at Jack's sleeve and informed him that just like the bass, the pats were also out of season. Jack ignored this, saying that Duffy wouldn't be back. They'd make fine table fare and no one would ever know.

And Duffy didn't return. We fooled around the camp fire most of the morning, returned to ice fishing—where on the way to our ice holes I slipped and fell. The ax I was carrying flew into the air and came down squarely on my right hand, smashing my thumb. If one of the blades had hit, I'd have most likely lost part of my hand.

And that's how our campout and fishing trip ended—with me in mortal pain and in need of a visit to the local doctor. So we packed things up, including several dozen fish we'd caught the day before, plus Jack's four grouse, and trudged back through the snow.

A sudden jerk on my rod tip brought me back to the reality that I was on Murray Lake, not Cashion Lake, and that all that was then and this today. So I hauled up the large bass, looked at it longingly and booted it back into the hole. Then I packed up my fishing gear and sloshed back to lakeside and my truck. Duffy or not Duffy, I wasn't going to chance it this time.

Conservation officers don't seem to be as forgiving now as perhaps they were back in the old days.

Fish are wherever they're found.

Just A Minute on 'Dumb' Brook Trout

I fish for trout in particular—rainbow, brown and brook trout. And, I'm going to tell you somewhat of a secret of one of those species.

You see, I discovered long ago that while brown and rainbow trout are very smart, the 'brookie' seems to be about the dumbest fish in the river.

It all goes back to a time when my father raised those three species for the (then) Michigan Department of Conservation; raised millions of 'em, in fact. However, my dad was not a minister, nor a fly fisherman, and never gave a hoot about a river that ran through the property over rocks that were there since the basement of time.

But yes, a river really did run through one side of his 18 trout ponds, and its waters were shunted off at various locations to force fresh water into his ponds and keep the fingerlings-to-legal size trout alive.

No, back in those days the legal length for trout was seven inches, and a fisher could keep as many as 25 in a single day....provided they could catch that many. The river that ran along-side the ponds usually contained lots of native fish, along with those that occasionally escaped in high water or complete floods. And perhaps needless to say, I and my young fishing buddies swamped our moms' refrigerators with trout whenever a flood came through.

But eventually we found something even more exciting to do than to wait for Mom Nature to flood the ponds so we could catch the escapees, or to even fish the stream on a nice summer day.

Here's how it worked…About every two weeks during the summer a Conservation hatchery truck would pull in to be loaded up with legal-size trout, and my dad and his three employees would net the legals from a pond or two and pour them into tanks on that truck. Then the truck would take off for parts unknown, or so the guys in the truck thought.

Aha! Then came our plan. I, along with pals Sam, Jack and Tom, would jump into Mom's old World War II Jeep, fishing rods along, and secretly follow the hatchery truck.

The truck would soon wind down some old two-track to places where its driver and helper would get out alongside a river or stream. Then they'd proceed to pour several hundred fish into the water. Finally, they'd move on to another fish planting location, the location of which soon became no secret to us kids.

At some fishing holes they'd plant only rainbow, brown or brook trout, and in others they'd release all three species.

And here's the reason I mentioned earlier that the brook trout seems to be the dumbest fish in the stream. In a place where all three species are released, the rainbows and browns almost immediately dispersed up and down the stream. But not the brookies. Nope. They'd remain right there in the same hole and hit any hook that hits the water. We could stand right there and catch almost every one of them if we wanted to do so. Yes, we figured they were just plain dumb.

Now, should anyone attempt to do likewise and go following a hatchery truck, there is something I should mention. A brook trout, especially when raised on hatchery food (of course, back then it was ground-up horsemeat, not pellets), will be somewhat soft and not nearly as tasty as a wild brookie, or even a hatchery-raised brown or rainbow.

So good luck trying to eat 'em!

An Eight Pound Brook Trout?

I was on a business trip during summer in northern Michigan, and not too far from East Jordan when I decided to take a side road to town rather than follow the main drag.

The paved yet somewhat rough road wound gently through some hills. Suddenly I spotted a small stream passing beneath the roadway. I always keep an eye out for such likely fishing spots.

My fishing frenzy rose instantly, so I parked the vehicle and removed my tattered business coat. Then I retrieved one of my fly rods, which are always not far from my fingers. Quickly I picked out an old Queen of the Waters trout fly, assembled the rod, and headed for the little stream—no waders, no net, no extra anything did I take.

Just above the road was a small waterfall with a fair-sized pool below it. Sneaking down to the water's edge, I cast the fly out, just below the waterfall. Just one cast, and all dickens broke loose!

The largest brook trout (yes, I said brook trout) that I or anyone else around those parts had probably ever seen rose clear above the water and snapped up that fly. Yes, I know a brookie when I see one, and this one had to be at least an eight-pounder!

With the thought of a possible state record fish swimming around in my mind, I fought the tackle buster for all of five minutes as it doubled my rod in all directions around that pool. Once it even tried to gain the waterfall, but didn't make it. Then, in final action, it made a run into the corrugated pipe that passed beneath the roadway, and SNAP! That was it.

I stood there for several minutes, wondering if what had happened had actually taken place. But the ache in my right elbow and the missing Queen of the Waters fly finally proved that it had happened.

What? No such thing as an eight-pound brook trout, you say? Well now, let me relate a little item that occurred way back in the year of 1902.

Senator William Frye was an ardent lover of fishing, and in the far recesses of the woods he built a cabin, to which he traveled annually to spend his vacation plying the waters.

Once, upon his return from an outing, he met up with a naturalist named Dr. Agassiz and described an exciting experience he'd had. "Among my triumphs," he said proudly, "was the capture of a brook trout that weighed fully eight pounds."

Dr. Agassiz replied, "Reserve that for that circle of rod and reel celebrants, but spare the feelings of a sober scientist."

"This is no campaign whopper I'm telling," said Frye. "I weighed the trout and it was an eight-pounder!"

"The creature you caught could not have been a speckled trout," said Agassiz. "All the authorities on ichthyology would disprove your claim."

Senator Frye then replied, "I'll wager that it will not be long before you alter your textbook."

The following season found the statesman at his usual avocation, and one day he landed a brookie that weighed nine pounds. He packed the trophy in ice and sent it to Dr. Agassiz. A few days later he received a telegram that read: "The science of a lifetime kicked to death by a fact.—Agassiz."

So there, my friends. If you didn't believe my account about the whopper brook trout, maybe you'll take a fact from history. And if that isn't good enough, I can show you the very spot where I almost landed my eight-pounder!

If we go, we'll take it seriously and take a net along this time, along with one of my Queen of the Waters trout flies…After all, a good trout fly never lies, does it?

Distance Fly Casting Made Simple: Don't Do It!

S o, you attended one of those fly-fishing sessions where some masterful expert showed you how to fling 90 to 100 foot of fly line while merely gripping the rod lightly in one hand. Eh?

And maybe at first you were really impressed, but then discovered that the expert had tied a 6-ounce mousie on the end of the line and it hauled the fly line out as though a bell sinker was attached.

Then perhaps you may have noticed that rather than letting you use his Orvis with the mousie attached and thus able to repeat his wondrous cast, he handed you an old 7-foot glass rod with a No. 18 fly attached at the end of a curled line.

Well now, maybe that wasn't the exact experience you encountered at a fly-flinging session. But it was mine, and some years ago. But you know, at the time I really didn't care about achieving that magical touch, and I've never, that I can recall, seen my backing line go zipping through the guides as my fly zoomed out to 100 feet.

However, come to think of it, I never wanted to high jump 7 feet, broad jump 25 feet, or run a mile in under 4 minutes, either.

But now, with all that said, I'd better admit something. I really have wanted to be able to distance cast a fly line, so at a younger age I did take some lessons. But cast 90-100 feet? No, as I've always seemed to have less-than-perfect timing, often finding the fly stuck in an arm or even my hat, with strange knots in the line as well.

Ah, but one day I had an experience that may have finally cured me of the desire to show other fishermen my grandiose long-casting, fly-flipping prowess.

As luck would have it, I was fishing a wide stretch of the Pere Marquette River with a couple of doctor friends from Grand Rapids, and the 'luck' part of it was that should I get a fly caught in an ear, they'd surely know how to handle the situation.

That morning I began as though I really knew what I was doing, and a favorable wind at my back helped as I zoomed that fly out and almost to the other shore. It was nearly 100 feet, and I was really impressed with myself as I kept moving along while spraying that shoreline.

Ah, but no fish!

And then came the ultimate putdown. Suddenly I heard a shout, "Fish on!" and another "I got one on too!" And looking back I saw both guys I'd come with standing near the shore's edge, rods doubled over and each with a steelhead on line.

What a dope I'd been! They'd been castin' but 10-20 feet from shore, and right where I had been standing when first I entered the water. Yeah, I'd probably been walking on fish and never realized it.

So it was a frustrating experience and a lesson I'll never forget. But it wasn't over yet, as I turned upstream and began to cast within my, shall we say, 50-foot limit or so. Thus, I too had some success, landing and releasing a couple of dandy steelies, caught within a distance I was actually capable of reaching.

But future distance fly-flinging lessons? Na, they're out the window now, and I've even stopped looking at those books and tapes showing young kids as they effortlessly zoom a fly out to 100 feet.

Well, I have made one sly move, at that. I simplified distance casting by cutting about 20 feet off the back of my fly line. Now, other fishermen I'm around, being none the wiser, seem to approve of my 'distance' casting. And oh, I've also stopped walking through or over fish as I try reaching a distant shoreline. You might say, for greater success, I'm standing a little closer to my targets!

Flies Float and Sinkers Stink

An acquaintance of mine was a charter boat captain on Lake Michigan for many years. Since he quit the charter business, he's owned a small lure and sinker manufacturing business. He has operated it out of an old building and on the main floor. He has living quarters on the second floor.

Well now, I walked in on good ol' Carl one afternoon, unannounced, of course. Walked in? That's hardly an appropriate way to put it. He lives and works alone, so what you find is a bachelor's mess along with a hodge-podge of old machinery and used equipment.

Entry is by way of an unmarked side door, then one need be careful not to step on the tail of one of several cats that wait just inside to pounce outside when the door is opened.

Once inside you must adjust your eyes to the dimness. (I'll wager that Carl's electric bill is almost nothing.) Then you wind your way around several old Queen Mary pieces of equipment to where you can eventually make out a figure huddled intensely over a drawing board.

That figure of course is Carl, laying out designs for either a new lure, a bell sinker, or even some new 'what not.'

Carl glances up as you stumble over a stack of lead ingots, but doesn't move. "Grab a couple of cans of suds out of the fridge over there," he sort of orders.

By this time it was late in the afternoon, so I did as told and handed Carl one as I cracked open the other can.

"Haven't seen you around for a while, Ed," he says as he peers over glasses that are about ready to slip off his nose. "What's up? You owe me money or something?"

Having seated myself on an old drafting stool stage left, I replied, "Matter of fact, I do owe you some money. You recall that batch of sinkers you heated up for me last summer? Well, I'm here to pay off."

Carl's heavyset form rippled as he turned to chuckle, "Well it's about time. Heck, I thought you'd drowned off Grand Haven or somewhere."

"Hardly," I said matter-of-factly. "So how's the lure and sinker business going?"

Carl took a long sip of suds and then wiped his mustache with his hand before answering. "Look around. Does this place look like Rapala, Fenwick or Garcia to you?"

"Nope," I said, "what it looks like to me is one man's passion and persistence though. That has to count for something, doesn't it?"

"Hey, that's good of you to say such," he remarked, grinning like a butcher's dog, "Then how about buying some more lures and sinkers from me, eh?"

"Carl, you know I mostly fly fish. Besides, a fly floats and gloats while a sinker sinks and stinks…Well anyway, that's the way I mostly look at it. And you know what I think? I think you should try to sell this place to one of those big companies. The sort of stuff you're making sold to the tune of several billion dollars in the states last year alone. Those big companies have been buying up every similar small business in sight. Maybe you should contact them."

Carl coughed on some suds and replied, "None of those big companies would be interested in my Mickey Mouse operation. Besides, what would I do during the off season when I'm not operating the boat?"

Well, ol' Carl had me there, so I handed him a $20 check to pay for those nearly-forgotten sinkers. He eyed the check carefully and at length, presumably to see if it was the real thing, then folded it about six times and stuffed it into a torn shirt pocket.

I got up to leave and fired off one last salvo.

"I'll get some more lures from you another time, Carl. In the meantime, just remember that flies float and sinkers stink!"

He grinned and tossed an old, rusty lure in my direction. I grabbed it, along with a little pain from the rusty hooks. Then I turned and made an exit, stage right, as I remarked, "Like a famous man once said, 'I shall return'".

The Old Badger Game—
with a Real Badger

I'm certain there are many different 'there-I-was-holding-the-bag' scenarios. Just not many about badgers.

There's the one that happens in some inner cities, where you can drive 20 miles or more and never leave the scene of the crime—where some robber who just held up a bank is left holding the bag in front of the police.

And there's the old college fraternity bit where a freshman pledge is driven miles out into the woods, handed a bag of 'survival' stuff and is left to find his way out of there. Of course, what he finally discovers is that he's been clutching a bag of dirty sweat socks.

Sure, there's also the old 'snipe hunt' where a youngster is given a gunny sack and is told to sit in a certain spot in the woods, sprinkle a few peanuts about, and wait to bag a snipe. Of course the rest of the 'hunting' party never take up positions but quietly retire to a VFW post to entertain themselves.

Indeed there are many versions of being left holding the bag. However, I believe the one my older brothers once pulled on me could top 'em all. It also got a little dangerous.

We were living, or was it simply existing, on an old 80-acre farm north of Petoskey, and I was around the age of 8. Approximately a third of our land was wooded with oak trees, and there were also those sugar maples where I'd tip up the sap buckets and drink the sweet nectar on my way to and from school in the spring.

In those woods were a variety of animals, none the least of which were the badgers…And therein lay the rub, for they were nasty critters that lived in large dens in the meadows along the woods. And, due to their ferocity, my brothers, Don and Ross, generally left them alone. But not always, as I was to discover.

Time and again I'd pleaded with my brothers to take me on one of their many hunts, to no avail. Then one early morning they somewhat mischievously informed me that they were about to embark on a badger hunt, and that I could tag along.

My older brother Don handed me a feed sack and dad's old double-barrel shotgun. So, with that heavy 12-gauge shotgun and the sack slung over a shoulder, I trailed after the two worthies, with not the slightest inkling of what I was in for.

In the side of a bank hear the woods we came across a large badger den. And I watched as Ross took my sack and placed it carefully over the entrance to the den. He then weighed its edges down with rocks.

"Now what?" I asked, sort of wide-eyed.

"Well," Ross replied, 'you perch yourself over there on that stump. Pretty soon that badger will come running out and land right in that sack—that's when you'll shoot 'em."

"But what if I miss?" I asked, as brother Don stuck two shells into my gun, worked the safety and handed it back.

"Miss? How can you miss?" he said. "Both barrels are loaded and I'd recommend that you fire off both of 'em…That old badger won't have a chance."

So they left me there, sitting on that stump and shaking with what should have been anticipation, but was not, and they quietly disappeared over the bank and out of sight.

I raised the gun several times, aiming it at the sack and flipping the safety on and off. I'd surely be prepared…Well, I wasn't.

Now then, the truth of the matter is that I was not yet woods-wise enough to know that a badger also has a back door to its den, as do many animals. And I also didn't know that this one's back door was located on the other side of that bank.

Suddenly a shot rang out as one of my brothers fired his gun into the other door of that badger's den. I flew off the stump and upright, scared to death. Then that bag was filled with a jumping, scrambling and snarling ball of fury, actually edging toward me as the badger fought to get out.

Well now, I had a death-grip on that shotgun and both barrels suddenly discharged, probably peppering the heck out of the neighbor's cows. I landed several feet away on my rump, scrambled to my feet and stood there petrified. Then another shot rang out and the bag stopped moving. And looking up, there were my brothers looking down from the top of the knoll and howling with laughter.

"So how'd you enjoy your first badger hunt?" asked Don, amid their laughter.

"Maybe...well, maybe...I shouldn't have come along," I finally stammered.

Then Ross walked down and carefully took my gun away. "We were right here all the time," he smiled, "but I guess it's been a shocking time for you." Then he winked toward Don and said, "We'll take you along on some future hunts, but there's just one thing—if you ever tell Dad or Mom about this badger hunt, next time you won't be holding the bag, you'll be in it."

And I've since been very careful about telling anyone about my first, and only, badger hunt.

Rowdy, Wilder Than a March Hare

Writer's note: Most of us have owned several dogs, or at least one, that we grew to love over the years. I've owned many, some who actually owned me. I want to tell you about one of those that probably owned me.

I discovered the shivering pup one morning when I came in from running my trap line. He was lying on a bale of straw, looking up at me with huge, brown eyes.

I have no idea where he came from. The thin and ragged puppy simply arrived at our haven in the woods one early winter and took up residence in our one-stall garage. The run-down outbuilding had been without a door for many years, and Mom's old World War II Jeep, the one that I often, at the age of 12, rode over the hills and across the streams, was parked there amid a bevy of old tool boxes and a clutter of garden equipment.

From the pup's looks he could have been part pointer, setter or hound—more hound than anything else, I guessed. He was predominately black and white, and his long, black tail whipped about several times at sight of me.

I dropped a couple of frozen muskrats to the floor, and he gave no protest as I lifted him up and carried him inside the house.

There was no protest from the dog, that is. Different words came from mom and dad.

"Where did you find that mangy pup?"

"We don't need a dog around here. Besides, he looks wilder than a March hare."

"There's a war on and it's one more mouth to feed."

"Well, maybe we can keep him for a few days 'til we can find a good home for him."

The final statement came from mom, who was to ferret out some leftovers and a dose of milk. The pup gulped it all down.

And now, as commentator Paul Harvey would have said, the rest of the story.

The puppy simply grew on all of us, and after two weeks I knew it would never need another home. Even dad softened at the little pup's rowdy activity, as it began to follow him about his daily chores of feeding and caring for the fish in our several trout ponds. And it was dad who named him Rowdy.

So Rowdy rapidly became accustomed to his new home, bouncing about it like a ping-pong ball and giving out humor like a comic. He slept alongside my bed at night, only waking me occasionally for a quick trip outside. He needed no toilet training.

Rowdy grew stronger and larger over those first weeks, and I began to let him run the trap line with me. It wasn't much of a line, winding about a half-mile up and down the Pere Marquette River and with about 30 trap sets. Sometimes we'd get one or two muskrat a day, sometimes none, but the pelts were paying for school clothes.

Now, as many are aware, muskrat traps aren't really made to hold raccoons. But one early morning we came across one in a trap. I had drowning sets, but the raccoon had just been caught and was floundering in the water.

Rowdy plunged wildly into the water and toward the raccoon, and suddenly I remembered something dad had told me—a raccoon will actually drown a dog by getting on its head and holding it under the water.

I carried an old single shot bolt action .22, one dad allowed me to take while on the trap line. Rowdy was almost to the animal when I raised the gun and fired, not even considering the worth of the raccoon pelt. The raccoon stopped floundering, and Rowdy made no attempt to grab it. He came to my call.

Yes, dad said the pelt was ruined by the shot, but mom took one look at the animal and said if I'd skin it out she'd cook it. Well I did and she did, and it tasted pretty good, although never had she offered to cook up one of my 'rats'.

So my wild Rowdy grew, and I did too. Over the ensuing years we hunted small game together, although he never was a good bird dog. Anything that flew would be scattered well ahead, as at the sight of a game bird he'd take off like a mouse to its hole. But squirrels? Now that was a different story, for Rowdy soon discovered that a squirrel would edge over to the opposite side of a tree. So he'd run over there, causing the rodent to edge to my side for a clean shot. We filled mom's larder with a lot of squirrels.

Rabbits? I soon discovered that Rowdy needed to be called off one if it escaped my first shot. Early on he'd taken off after one and didn't return until nightfall. Not good.

Rowdy was my faithful companion through high school, eagerly awaiting my afternoon returns and sometimes traveling the half mile to meet me at the schoolhouse door. Everyone in our small hamlet knew him by sight and name, and he was a happy camper.

It was a sad day when I finally went off to college, leaving Rowdy behind. Then another war followed and I was caught up in that for a few years.

But it was an even sadder day when I finally returned home to be told that Rowdy had recently been killed by a car while returning home from the old schoolhouse, where he'd waited for me years before. We had spent but four years of the eight together, but he was the companion of my youth.

Many years have passed, but I sometimes look down beside my bed, hoping to see those big, brown eyes looking back. They don't, of course, for my old and faithful companion is no longer there.

Queen, Rowdy and Jack

A recent walk through the old forest began with a mere whim to revisit one of the areas where I'd hunted as a kid.

It was a place I hadn't visited for almost 50 years, but one destined to take on a nostalgic twist.

I began along a path that was now overgrown with brush, eventually winding my way through to an old, narrow, wooden bridge over a small stream. I hesitated and moved carefully over the planks that were badly deteriorated. Once on the other side, more tangles of brush eventually gave way to a sandy bank, and that bank stopped me in my tracks.

You see, somewhere at the bottom of that bank were the graves of several dogs I owned during those many years ago. That was where Queen, Rowdy and Jack now lay.

I hesitated several moments before climbing the bank to enter the woods. However, upon taking but a few steps into the woods of pine and oak, memories came flooding back.

Just ahead was a swale where Queen had cornered and flushed my first partridge. She was a young English setter then and was just as surprised and as happy as this young hunter to gather up her first wild bird, which she was quite reluctant to have taken away from her mouth. We'd hunted that swale and many other places throughout the forest ahead during the several years that followed.

I walked onward through the swale and into a swampy area with a small creek running through it. This was a place where Rowdy and I'd once chased many a rabbit through the pine trees and mud, defeated more often than not but sometimes able to scare up an evening meal.

Rowdy was a tan and white hound and middle-aged when my father, then an employee of the Conservation Department (now the Michigan Department of Natural Resources), had caught the dog chasing a deer and hauled him home for some additional training.

I guess such training was my job. I was forced to call him off deer tracks on several occasions. One of those I well remember.

It was bowhunting season for deer. I'd taken proudly to the woods with a new bow and several arrows I'd jammed into a homemade quiver. I hadn't looked behind until I was in this same swampy area. But suddenly Rowdy, who'd been sneaking along behind, stepped ahead of me and headed for a huge pine stump.

I stopped now during my walk. There, just ahead of me, was that very stump. The memory flooded back.

A large doe had been lying beside that stump. As Rowdy and I approached, she'd risen up slowly, just watching us. I raised my bow and fired an arrow, never even coming close. The firing of that arrow from only about 20 feet away from her, along with Rowdy's approach, finally got her sleepy attention and off she went, tail high and with Rowdy in rapid pursuit.

The upshot of it was that I didn't corral that dog for several hours. When I finally did find him, it was nearly necessary to help him home. He was totaled out, but there was one consolation. I never saw him chase another deer after that.

So I hiked onward, along the creek bank and up to a bluff that looked out over the main river. There I began to think of Jack. He was a black and white hound and setter mix who hadn't really been much of a hunter, but who'd camped out with me on this same bluff on many summer nights.

Jack had been more of a pet and house dog as well as my camping buddy. You know, the type that walks a kid to school in the morning and then lies down to wait for that kid to come out that schoolhouse door in the afternoon. He too was a great pal.

So finally there I was, standing at the end of what had been the end of my hunting trail so many years ago. As I looked down from the bluff to the river, it almost seemed as though the water was reflecting the images of Queen, Rowdy and Jack.

I guess images such as those never die. No, they remain with us as long as we live.

The 'Dog' Days of Autumn

I believe that autumn is always coming on and that you hunters with dogs are always on deck…That it may be time to load up your dogs with carbohydrates and check out the shotguns, as small game seasons are approaching when we can go after some cottontails, fox or gray squirrel, woodcock, grouse, or even pheasants.

And among those hunting dogs waiting on deck will be pointers, flushers, retrievers, and even some in-betweeners that we often find to be the best hunting stock.

All of those dogs, just as you and I, come with varying amounts of intelligence, as well as size and shape.

Those of you with a Chesapeake, Labrador or golden will most likely have the best retrievers, and some of you may have to work out beforehand in order to keep up with your wide-ranging pointer or setter. Well, for me I prefer a spaniel for the max in a flushing dog.

Now, you've probably guessed that I'm leading up to something here. And yes, there's a little story I'd like to relate concerning pheasant hunting. (Following that we'll get into a discussion about hunting dogs in more detail.)

Seems there were two casual friends, let's call 'em John and Doug. Both were avid pheasant hunters, yet seldom did they hunt together.

Well, the two happened to come across each other at a local bistro, around noon on the opening day of pheasant season.

John was looking down at his dirty boots in some despair, and he remarked to Doug, "We worked three different fields this morning and

94

my dog didn't find a single bird. Guess there aren't any pheasants this year."

"Well now, that is a shame," Doug answered. "My dog put up four birds and I knocked two of 'em down."

"Where'd you hunt, over at the pheasant farm?" asked John.

Then Doug bragged that where they hunted never seemed to matter. So he threw out a challenge. "Tell you what we'll do. We'll go hunt those same three fields you hunted this morning, and we'll get some birds. You'll see. My dog's got the best nose for birds there ever was."

John's bluff was called, so he half-heartedly accepted. Thus it was that the two went out to the first of those three fields that John and his dog had hunted. In rapid order, Doug's pointer barked twice and stood at point; whereupon they flushed two roosters and bagged them both.

Then they proceeded to the second field, where a similar thing took place. Doug's dog barked three times, and in short order they'd flushed and bagged another pheasant. John was really in awe at the proceedings.

Now then, at the third field they loosed the dog, whereupon it began to bark repeatedly while hopping about like a frog in a foolish frenzy. Finally, the dog grabbed up a large stick and shook it about furiously as it jumped up and down between the hunters.

John scratched his head in utter disbelief. "What in the world is that all about?" he asked.

Doug watched his dog a moment longer, then he turned to his companion with an ear-to-ear grin. "I told you he was the best," he said. "My dog is telling us that there are more froggin' pheasants in this field than you can shake a stick at!"

Well now…

Since Doug's dog was a pointer, let's discuss those a moment.

The pointer, originally used for horseback trails, is more of a wide-ranging dog. However, over the years he's been trained into a medium-to-close range dog. I guess that's because that for eons most of us have hunted on foot rather than on a horse.

But, while the pointer is the best known of the pointing breed, other fine ones include the English setter, the Weimaraner, and of course the Brittany spaniel. The Brittany is the smallest of the lot, but seems the easiest to train.

The English springer spaniel seems to be the ultimate in a flushing dog. Its webbed feet and heavy bone structure also make it ideal for swimming or working in wet terrain. But I can tell you from experience that it is a hoot to train!

The cocker spaniel, which can become an excellent hunter, is now so inbred that it is primarily a pet or a show dog. However, I once had one that was the exception and an excellent hunter as well as the ultimate in a companion.

For retrievers, the Labrador seems to be the most popular upland game bird dog in America. Especially so for waterfowl hunters. And the golden retriever is of superior intelligence, having a nose for game that is hard to beat. Chesapeake Bay retrievers, relatives to the Labrador, are rough-water dogs and can take extreme cold better than most dogs.

So, if you're in the hunt for a good hunting dog, there you have it—"hunting" is the key word. So buy a dog from a good sire and dame that are good hunters. For if you procure one that stems from a line of house pets, you may wind up like John in the story above—by owning a great house pet, but where "no nose is not good news."

Pheasants Today, Mr. Chips, and the Old Stump Row

Early, traditional pheasant hunting during the 1930s in places like South Dakota, or even Michigan, were more of a large group activity than today.

Now, we usually pheasant hunt with a close friend or two, or even alone or with our dog. And most of us don't go much for larger areas of cover, during the regular or the winter hunt. Roosters will make fools of us there. Rather, we go for cover such as fence rows, abandoned farm areas, or overgrown ditches and old stump rows. Those areas we can hunt alone or with a small hunting party.

And today we need to be more of a sneak. For example, I've found that if I quickly advance a few yards through a likely pheasant area, and then pause for a few moments, I can get right up on 'em. In that way the birds will gradually become more nervous and eventually flush. Also, in slim cover a pheasant will hold longer for a dog and a hunter.

Regardless, roosters seem to always have an escape plan, which they implement as the pressure increases. They run and sneak more and the approach for a good shot becomes more difficult. So the hunter needs to be sneaky and at the ready.

That old stump row I mentioned earlier reminds me of a particular hunt I had several years ago with my dog, Mr. Chips. It was winter and we weren't pheasant hunting. In fact, there was no winter pheasant season then and we were after some cottontails.

We had just by-passed an old row of stumps and about to enter a likely looking hedgerow when I thought I heard something, stopped, and glanced back along the stumps. Mr. Chips had also turned, and he wasn't pointing but just sniffing and looking intently at the stumps. I saw nothing, but decided to investigate.

I approached the area carefully, then Mr. Chips moved ahead in a quick walk. Suddenly a ringneck went up from under the protection of a large tipped-up stump, his flapping wings making the snow swirl in the crisp morning air and the sun turning it into a dozen or more tiny, dazzling rainbows.

I watched as the beautiful bird went out a ways, then leveled off to come to a gliding rest in some corn stubble about a hundred yards off. Beautiful, I thought, as I started away again. But after a few steps I realized that Mr. Chips hadn't followed my lead. Turning, I saw that he was instead continuing to edge up on that old stump, while sniffing the ground with his short tail moving his butt like an egg beater.

Then suddenly another rooster took flight, and another, and still another. I stood in awe with my 16-guage pointed downward and watched as no less than nine pheasants—everyone a beautiful rooster— flew out and away from under that old stump. For a moment I felt like the guy who'd put instant coffee in the coffee pot by mistake and later wondered where the grounds went! … Nine ringnecks, and not a single hen in the bunch! And NO winter pheasant season.

Mr. Chips turned about then and looked at me, big brown eyes in total dismay as though asking, "Well, I found them. Why didn't you shoot?" I patted the dog and said, as though he understood every word, "Old boy, it's too bad we can't find a bonanza like that during pheasant season. Come on, let's see if we can locate a cottontail or two."

Man's Best Friend, ad infinitum

Nothing much remains of my old hunting cabin today. Just the long walking trail to get into it, the wind in the pines, the dust devils swirling over the groundhog dens around its burned out shell, and of course, the old pump handle standing defiantly in a corner.

Standing there catching my wind from the hike, I remembered when the area was alive with people and dogs—the many dogs I'd had with me over the years.

These memories and more flooded back one summer as I took what I considered to be a necessary hike into the old property with my aging spaniel, Mr. Chips. "Chipper" was 12 and ailing from poor eyesight and hearing along with a painful back.

It was going to be our last visit to the cabin together.

As I stood there steeped in nostalgia, Mr. Chips was trying once again to playfully attack one of the dust devils, and I could not help but be reminded of the many dogs who'd done the same over the myriad of years.

Roudy had been the first, a large Brittany who'd shared nine years at the cabin. Then there was Old Jack, the pointer-setter mix with the broken front foot that had mended somewhat grotesquely only to become stronger than the others. Jack had been my constant companion during 11 years of hunting from the cabin. That one had a nose for game that never failed him or me.

Ah, Queenie. She had been the shy English setter and the last until Mr. Chips. She was first and foremost a lady, and she'd let you know it, and was also the top hunter until Mr. Chips came along. However, she'd been just one of the parade of many faithfuls that had circled and curled up on the old braided rug, and lay there with huge, brown eyes turned upward toward a beloved master.

I was caught up in one of those sudden trips down Memory Lane. There was no denying it, and as I poked about the old burnt shell of the cabin, the memories flooded through me.

I recalled the cold November day that Louie, Steve, Walt (old hunting partners) and I had lugged an old pool table all the way in from the two-track. That pool table offered some of the great times we all had—as the days were filled with hunting and the evenings full of pranks and fun.

For example, there was the time when Steve had bagged his first buck, a 10-pointer, and had awakened the following morning to discover a family of field mice nesting in one of his hunting boots. Louie and I knew how they got there, but we never told.

There had been another auspicious occasion when several of the younger members of our hunting party had been unceremoniously entertained by a bunch of curious, loud, yet somehow not too ferocious "bears" that managed to prowl the exterior of the cabin from dusk to dawn. Again, Louie and I never told.

Then suddenly I was recalling the many youngsters that had been with us at the cabin, some in their now-I-look-like-you-dad hunting attire and others in jeans and checkered shirts—sons and daughters of mine and past hunting partners. Those had been good times, but they were over.

Mr. Chips was barking at a squirrel, snapping me out of my melancholy. Distastefully I then recalled the reason I'd trekked to the cabin with my dog. He would now be laid to rest with Roudy, Old Jack and Queenie.

I looked to my gun.

Mr. Chips sat beside the pine tree, looking first at me with those huge brown eyes and then up at the chattering squirrel as if to say, "Well, are you going to get that squirrel or not?"

I raised the gun and sighted it, my eyes beginning to blur. Quick and easy and it would be all over. No more pain and suffering for Chipper.

I lowered the gun. I couldn't do it—just as I was unable to do so with Roudy, Jack and Queenie.

Mr. Chips is still with me, and very well-cared for. Fact is, he's pampered and spoiled more than ever, and will remain that way as long as possible. You see, a friend like Mr. Chips is just like a cabin that is no longer, yet will always be.

After Chipper I may never own another dog. Then again, perhaps there is always another dog—sort of like that old saying someone once told me:

> All big dogs have little dogs
> To worry and to bite 'em,
> And little dogs have littler dogs,
> And so ad infinitum.

There is an ending to it all. Of the Brittanies, pointers and setters I've owned—each a marvelous animal in its own right—Mr. Chips topped them all. And he, for the worth of it, is not an American water spaniel. He is a large *cocker* spaniel.

A Final "Goodbye" to Mr. Chips

I awoke with a start, managing to jerk the steering wheel of the Ranger just in time to avoid several oak trees along the two-track leading in to the old cabin.

I'd driven north to the hunting camp in late evening and was bone tired. Parking the truck and shutting down the engine and lights, I leaned my head forward to the steering wheel and dozed off again.

Suddenly, my spaniel Mr. Chips whined and began to lick the side of my face, bringing me out of my stupor.

"Need to go outside, Mr. Chips?"

My faithful companion pranced his paws anxiously on the seat. He knew the word "outside" and needed to do just that.

Mr. Chips was now 14, and ailing somewhat from poor eyesight and hearing along with a painful arthritic back. But he'd been my best buddy all these years and to admit that I doted over him would be a minor statement.

"Okay boy," I said as I opened the truck door and let him lower himself gingerly from the cab. "We've got to get inside and get a fire going anyway. It's gonna be a cold one tonight."

Now, I've never figured it unusual to converse with Mr. Chips, or with any of the dogs that have owned me, for that matter. When a dog becomes a constant companion it becomes no less than a family member, and it's almost as though the animal can talk back.

Unlocking the cabin door, I swung it wide to let the cool evening air displace the musty odor of the cabin's interior. Mr. Chips soon joined me inside and looked on with tilted head as I lit an overhead gas light and started a fire in the old wood stove. Then he followed me to the kitchen, where I primed the old long-handled pump and drew water in several pans which I placed on the flat of the stove.

"There ol' buddy, maybe we can get some rest now." And thus said, I plopped into one of the several easy chairs that yawned openly near the stove.

Mr. Chips curled up on the braided rug at my feet and looked up at me with those huge, brown eyes, and then I suddenly found myself going down that old Memory Lane. For he was but one of the faithful dogs that had done likewise over the span of years...

Roudy had been the first: a large Brittany who'd shared nine years at the cabin. Then there'd been Old Jack, a pointer/setter mix who'd been my companion over an eight-year span. And ah, there was Queen, the shy English setter who'd been the last until Mr. Chips entered my life.

Then total nostalgia overcame me and other memories flooded to mind...I recalled the many hunting trips to the cabin, along with those I'd hunted with over the years. There'd been Louie, Ross, Steve, Walt, Bill and others who'd shared the great times. And then there were the many youngsters who'd tag along, some in their now-I-look-like-you dad hunting attire, and others in jeans and checkered shirts.

We'd pulled some pranks on the kids in those days. Such as on one auspicious occasion when some of the youngsters were unceremoniously "entertained" by some raucous and somewhat "ferocious" bears that prowled around outside the cabin from dusk to dawn. Or the time when one of the young boys awoke to find a nest of field mice in his hunting boots...And the fun times had gone on and on...

Mr. Chips stirred at my feet and I glanced down to see him still somewhat reposed, but with those huge brown eyes upturned as if asking, "Hunting today?"

I paused before speaking, thinking all too fondly of this dog—one who'd never given up on a hunt and had been at my side nearly every moment of every day for many years.

"Well, Mr. Chips," I said rather hesitantly, "This will probably be our last visit together at the cabin. You're really in a lot of pain, and I guess our hunting days together are at an end...But we've had lots of good times, both here and at home over the years…I know I'll never forget you."

Mr. Chips answered with a slight wag of his short tail and stared up at me as if to say, "It's OK, I understand."

Something startled me and I raised my head from the steering wheel of my truck. It was early dawn, but through the cab window I could see the burned-out shell of the old cabin—It had been destroyed by fire nearly a year earlier. Then, through the haze I could make out the old pump handle that now erupted from the ground, while the wind was whipping up over the groundhog dens around the foundation's perimeter.

Instinctively, I looked at the seat beside me. Mr. Chips was not there, and would not be ever again. I'd had him put to sleep several days earlier.

The cabin was gone now, and so was Mr. Chips. But I suddenly realized why I'd come here one last time. It wasn't about memories of the cabin; it was in memory of Mr. Chips.

I started the truck and swung it about with a heavy heart.

"This time it really is good-by, Mr. Chips," I uttered through trembling lips.

Déjà vu Becomes a 'Murphy' Law

Since I had to put my old "pheasant finder" Chips to sleep, I've shied away from owning another hunting dog.

Chipper was like a buddy and pal.

However, all that may change due to a recent happening.

A lady member of our church goes to the local Humane Society whenever she has the opportunity, and she "walks" dogs that are captive there. Seems she has tremendous empathy for animals, particularly dogs.

One Sunday she told me she'd been walking a Black Labrador-mix named Murphy, and it was a fine young dog with a great personality and much exuberance. She said if I were in the market for another dog, I should see this Murphy.

Well, I waved it off in my mind until a few days later when I happened to be near the animal shelter on business. Then, what she'd said suddenly sprang to mind, and sort of on a lark I turned in at the society entrance.

After making out a form that proved I had a good home for a dog and was somewhat seriously looking for one, I was given the number of Murphy's cage and was allowed to proceed into the kennel area.

If you've never visited such an area, I can tell you it was a heartfelt experience. I passed by many dogs on my way to Murphy's cage, and inside each were dogs of almost every mix or breed, each attempting to get my attention. Many barked or whined, and most of them came to me to lick my hand through the bars. It was as though they were pleading to be taken home. I talked to them, and most responded with lots of affection.

They'd said that Murphy's cage was near the end of the first aisle, and when almost there I noticed a beautiful black and white Springer Spaniel that was lying on his bed and looking up at me with saddened eyes. So, I stopped to look at his credentials, posted on the cage door. His name was Murphy!

"Well now," I said aloud, "you're certainly not a Black Lab, but your name is Murphy, all right."

At the sound of his name, the Springer suddenly sprang to life. He came up to me, prancing his feet, wagging his stubby tail, and laying his head against the bars. I petted him and began to talk to him. He reacted with what were almost lonesome whines and yips, and then reached down to his bed to retrieve a toy bone. He wanted to play, so I stayed with him for some time as we enjoyed each other's company.

Suddenly, another dog two cages down the aisle noticed the ruckus and came to the front of his cage. I looked, and there was indeed a Black Lab trying to grab my attention! I vacated the first cage and went over to him, and he reacted in a manner similar to the Springer I'd just left. Then, glancing at his credentials on the door, I discovered that this was the "Murphy" I'd originally intended to visit!

It was like déjà vu all over again.

"So there are actually two of you 'Murphys' in here," I remarked. "Well, maybe I've been visiting the wrong dog." And, upon hearing his name, the dog went into the same "take-me-home" routine as had the Springer Spaniel.

Yeah, it was somewhat of a quandary, for I couldn't even think of having both of them. And both were obviously fine, intelligent animals, perhaps a real blessing to any household.

I eventually said good-bye to both dogs and returned to the shelter office, telling them of my experience and that I'd need to think it over. They said both dogs had been there for some time, so I could take my time if I decided to take one of them home.

Well, I took my time, and a couple of weeks later when I took my wife in to see the "Murphys", they had both found homes. We were a little disappointed and said we'd come back and look again some day.

But disappointment wasn't my real reason for writing this column. Not at all. It is to encourage anyone who has the desire to own a dog, or even a second one, to visit their local Humane Society. Although they may not find one exactly to their liking, or not even leave with the "Murphy" that's on their mind, if they have a passion for pets, they are in for an unforgettable, heart-felt experience.

The gobbler had already seen me.

The Lying Tales of Getting One's First Turkey

I didn't turkey hunt when I was a lad, because back then there were none around Michigan to hunt. I began stalking the sharp-eyed longbeards about 11 years ago when they became plentiful up in my normal hunting area—north about 75 miles, left at the old oak tree, right at the pine stump fence until you reach ... Well, you know.

But the subject comes up, and often.

For example, several of my hunting buddies and I were sitting around quaffing a few glasses of suds at Nick Finks Grill and Saloon one evening when the subject of one's first turkey kill was broached. And that happened because Jake McBoom suddenly crowed that he felt lucky about this fall's turkey lottery.

We all sneered because Jake has a tremendous imagination. Rarely does he succeed at anything, let alone the lottery or an actual turkey kill.

But Jake's remark did open the box, and soon a plethora of remarkable accounts of turkey hunting expertise and outright lies began to spill forth.

Old "Blackpowder" Barrel led off. (I must explain here that we don't call him Blackpowder just because he always hunts with a muzzleloader. It's due to the fact that he rubs the powder all over his face and hands on opening morning, and doesn't wash it off until he gets the bird—which is eventually, and most likely, from his wife when he arrives home ...

But we are glad he's not a smoker—with all that powder on him, who knows?)

"My first bird was neigh unto a world record," said a straight-faced Blackpowder. "I'd staked out along his trail three mornings and when he finally came within range I saw that his beard was almost draggin' the ground. Well, I pulled him in real close with a couple of purrs and yelps, and suddenly he let out a gobble that shook every tree in the woods."

"I dispatched him when he got within 25 yards—weighed in at 34 pounds, with a 20-inch beard and two-inch spurs. Yessir, biggest gobbler I ever got or saw. Scored 250 Pope & Young points!"

"Pope & Young points?" we queried simultaneously, emitting grunts and sneers. But we questioned no further, all of us knowing old Blackpowder's ability to rubberize the truth. Besides, by that time he'd about had his limit, and not of birds.

So one by one, we expounded on our first turkey conquest. Smokey Feathers said he got his first longbeard when the thing flew from its roost one morning and landed square in his lap. He had subsequently, and not too gently, reached out and strangled the poor thing to death. No matter, and I'm quite certain no one had the audacity to later look it up in the rules, although someone muttered something or other about the legality of strangling a turkey to death.

Bush (Rear-view) Firewick wiped the suds from his moustache and simply admitted that in 12 years of turkey hunting he'd never got one. But his remark drew a guffaw from the gallery, as we all knew that two years hence he'd lined one up on a two-track road with his old Ford Ranger and unceremoniously ran it over. We also knew it'd landed him a $1,000 fine and three days of rest in the county lockup, as a DNR officer had been driving along right behind him! Rear-view Bushy never looks into a mirror—which may help to explain his grizzly looks. I've no idea why he even has mirrors mounted on his truck.

Well now, the stories continued until suddenly it went quiet and I noticed they were all looking at me. So I plopped my glass down rather gently on the table and said in a quiet voice, "You guys are never going to believe how I got my first gobbler."

"Yeah, well try us," came the unison cry, as though they were attending a church service.

So I proceeded to explain how my brother Ross and I had located a well-traveled turkey trail and some dusting areas about a quarter mile from the cabin, and how we'd planned our strategy well—him setting up in some thick brush on one side of the path, while I laid down on the other side behind a large log. We were about 60 yards apart as the turkey flies.

Then we proceeded to call, me with some soft purrs and a few yelps, while he gave out with some loud intimidating gobbles. And sure enough, a gobbler began to answer and to slowly move in for a closer look-see.

Three hens had come down the path first, and they were followed by a large tom with about an 18-inch beard. I told them how the hens peered sideways at Ross and then over in my direction, while the tom was quite curious, maybe seeking to find another hen for his harem. He'd make a threatening move toward Ross' gobbling, then retreat and perform a little dance toward me.

"How long does this go on?!" came a cry from the impatient gallery.

"Well," I sez," not long. I was laying down behind the big log an' just peering over the top when another gobbler—one I hadn't even noticed, suddenly plopped its head and neck over that log and looked me square in the eyes. Then he let out a gobble that almost made me run to the cabin to change my drillies!"

Looks of disbelief were now fired my way. "So, what'd you do?"

I raised my arms as though wielding a shotgun. "Well, I took that Remington 870 magnum and whopped him right between the eyes with its barrel! ... Yessiree, the first and biggest tom I ever got. Weighed in at just under 37 pounds, with a 24-inch beard, and sported three-inch spurs!"

And with that the quaffing broke up. But not before old Blackpowder glanced sideways in my direction and sneered, "Of all the low down, unlikely, lying tales about getting a first turkey, I like yours the best!"

Turkey 'Tale' Time

I guess the poultry breeders have all but perfected the growing and marketing of turkeys. And perhaps that could cause some folks to wonder why a hunter would force himself or herself to sit cramped up for hours on end, camouflaged from top to bottom, in all manner of weather, while trying to entice one of those sharp-eyed gobblers within shotgun range.

Seems as though a trip to the store would be easier.

Ah, but that's not it at all. It's that rush of adrenalin that one feels as a longbeard comes into view, just as it is with deer hunting, other game hunting or any shooting sport for that matter.

At least that's been my experience over the years, and sometimes hunting experiences even have added value.

Take the time I sat for hours in a cold rain, calling and waiting and waiting and calling. Well, one of those big fellows suddenly exploded out of a tree not ten feet over my head and scared several years of growth right out of me. I was so struck I never got my gun up!

On another occasion, a huge longbeard sat in a two-track road directly in front of my Ranger. It wouldn't move, so I actually thought about running over it. Well, I thought better about the situation and stopped, then looked in my rear-view mirror to discover a conservation officer who'd been tailing me! A close call, to say the least. So I honked the horn, watched the bird make an exit stage left, then waved and smiled at the CO and went on my way. (He didn't smile back.)

The best chance I ever had to harvest a wild turkey wasn't even during turkey season. It was during deer season and I was sitting in my blind on the opening morning of the firearms season. About a half hour prior to daylight I suddenly heard what surely was an entire herd of deer pawing and scratching the ground. They were all around me, nearly in a circle.

Well now, it was for certain I'd be able to take my choice of any deer I wanted when daylight came on. However, I was about to be really surprised. When I could finally make out what was out there, I found I was totally surrounded by a flock of at least 25 turkeys, scratching for acorns. There were a few longbeards in the flock too—however, right timing, wrong season!

You know, it seems that almost every paper or magazine you pick up about now is loaded with regulations, rules, the proper 'must-have' hunting equipment, and especially various turkey-hunting techniques. So, I'll not even get into such. Rather, the history behind wild turkeys may be appropriate, so we'll discuss some of that.

The wild turkey is considered to be the largest game bird native to North America. They were somewhat domesticated and bred by the Aztec and Suni Indians, who not only used them for food but in sacrificial ceremonies.

It is now believed that all varieties of turkeys throughout the world are descendants of this North American turkey, which came from Mexican stock. They were first sighted by Spanish conquerors around 1492, and somewhere around 1530 the Mexican species was taken back and introduced to Europe.

From the first American Thanksgiving, the turkey has been the traditional symbol of our American holiday, and it also came in a close second to the eagle as our national bird. Can you see a turkey on our folding money or coins? Just imagine the jokes that would conjure up today!

I do wish those who are hunting gobblers much success. But I caution any hunter not to go rushing toward those gobbling sounds you may hear…Remember, fools rush in while knowing turkey hunters sit tight and get soaked or freeze their bottoms off.

Deer Hunting 'Widows' Command Respect

Deer Camp U.S.A.—One of my deer hunting buddies, Chuck, and I made the northward trek in his 4 by 4. We were discussing deer and generalizing on the locations of same, when I chanced to notice Chuck's new cellular phone.

"Hey," I said, "your wife's over to my place so they'll know we're thinking of them too—not just abandoning them to deer hunt."

(Sounds like a great idea, eh? Read on.)

Chuck agreed, so I picked up the phone and dialed home. Gerri, my wife, answered, and I started to ask if all was OK when the phone suddenly went dead.

"It's been doing that sometimes," Chuck said. "I'm going to return that piece of junk and get a good one. Lay it down. Maybe we can call them later."

I put the phone down.

"They're probably doing fine," Chuck said. "Besides, they know what we're doing, and they know that they can trust us up there in the wild country." With that he turned and gave me a sly grin.

I laughed. "Ya," I said, "although, you know, there are lots of troubles and mischief a guy can find up around those small towns during deer season. A couple of us went into the VFW club last year and were swarmed by women wanting us to dance with them. Imagine that."

"Makes sense," replied Chuck. "Probably most of those women were deer hunters' wives—you know, widows of hunters who went—."

"North deer hunting," I broke in as we both looked at each other funny-like.

"Na," Chuck said after some silence. "They wouldn't do that… Maybe a—."

"Party," I injected. "With friends over?"

There ensued a doubtful moment of silence, then Chuck offered, "We'd better trust them, after all, they trust us. Besides, that little town near our camp, well, it's so slow and backward that one girl I heard about didn't have her sweet sixteen party until she was 38."

We both laughed, then I continued the thought. "I understand that she could have married any man she pleased. Problem was, she didn't please any of 'em."

More guffaws.

More silence.

Finally Chuck continued, "I hear a lot of women go out partying when their husbands are off deer hunting, but I doubt if Mary and Gerri would do that."

"Only if they went with a group of women—."

"Who dance with hunters in little towns up north," Chuck finished.

It's funny the sort of quandaries people can talk themselves into, and, needless to say, we were both contemplating the whole, disastrous situation. I could almost feel that Chuck was about to turn the truck around and head southward when I thought I heard a distant laughter.

The phone.

I picked up the receiver from its perch on the seat beside me, and there was hysterical laughter coming over it.

Our wives then explained that, in fact, the dead phone had come to life the moment I put it down. Both women had been listening to our entire conversation.

Of course we all had a good laugh over the incident, but my wife gave me a parting broadside just before we rang off.

"Now don't worry about us, dear," she said. "We'll be all right, and we'll find something to do... Oh, by the way, I almost forgot to ask—how long will you be up north, and when are you going again?"

I momentarily contemplated asking her why she wanted to know, but saw through her humor in time. Instead, I chuckled and told her we'd call again in a day or two.

We met up with my brother, Ross, and several of his hunting pards at the old cabin near the swamp. They were busily splitting some deadfall wood for the iron stove. I asked them what had happened to all the wood we cut last summer.

"It appears that someone backed a truck in here and made off with every cord of it." answered Ross. "Come on. We've got to get this done before tonight or we'll freeze."

"And oh, by the way," he continued, "I've some worse news for you. You know that 'Old Big Foot' deer you've been stalking for years, the one with the club foot?"

I nodded. I knew that deer like an old sock.

"Well, we found him yesterday. Dead, along old Wolf Lake road. Somebody got him with their truck, or car, or something... Big one, all right. And man, what a rack he had. Look up there." Ross then gestured over the cabin doorway, and there they had nailed up the 16-point rack of 'Old Big Foot' for all to see.

I stared at the rack for a moment, then looked away, blinking as I thought of all those years I'd stalked the old forest king.

"Not much use hunting now," I muttered under my breath. "Might just as well go dancing."

"What?"

"Might just have been a fancy," I replied. "I think I'll go call my wife."

Deer Hunt Was All About The Chase

I t was next to the last day of the regular firearms season. I parked the truck, charged the barrel of the old muzzleloader and carefully placed a cap under the hammer. Then I set out for my last hunt of the season.

A recent snowfall throughout the area had all but obliterated the trail I often use, and snow-laden branches of oak, pine and underbrush became obstacles as well as items of just plain beauty.

Proceeding as usual, I moved but a few steps at a time through the soft and soundless snow, pausing to look carefully in every direction. This is the manner in which I've normally deer hunted since the age of 12 or so, and while it has sometimes allowed me to sneak up on deer, most often it has not.

But as I shuffled carefully through the evening snow, I suddenly realized that getting a deer really wasn't a priority.

Rather, the woods were beautiful under a hazy western sun, and that old saying came once more to mind that the chase, rather than the conquest, was really the thing.

I chuckled to myself as I suddenly wondered if Will Shakespeare ever did much besides taking pen in hand, like fishing or hunting perhaps. Then I secretly grinned as I thought he must have at least fished—after all, didn't he make rods and reels?...Well, maybe not.

Finally, I paused for a time beside a fallen tree near an old deer trail. And as I waited there I not only realized that this was near the end of the season, but that God only knows what's going to happen in this millennium. Born in what is now called the "old school days," I'd never really expected to reach the end of the last century.

Those were dangerous years to grow up in—from part of the old depression era to nearly getting killed playing high school football with an old, leather helmet and little protection elsewhere as well. (We didn't win many games, but as we all said, we sure had a lousy time!) Then there was World War II and the Korean War. Thank goodness, I thought to myself, I was a tad old for the Vietnam War, or I'd likely not be here today enjoying the serenity of these woods.

But here I was, reminiscing over the past and wondering about the future.

I finally shuffled away from the old tree and continued along the snowy trail, questioning myself as to whether the 1900s had really been worth all the strife and misery that had encompassed our planet. Moreover, what would this new century bring?

Would it be the demise of those of us who still believe in a supreme being? Will computers rule the world rather than people? Will the distant planets and outer space really be explored?... Will those who follow in our footsteps be allowed to hunt or fish by the end of the year 2099?

My thoughts were suddenly interrupted by a slight crackling sound as I moved slowly around a bend in the trail near a large, snowy bush. I bent forward, peering around the bush, and there, not 20 feet away, stood a large buck—a six-pointer—browsing on some grass he'd discovered by pawing through the snow.

The deer was quartered away from me and hadn't detected my presence. In fact, it only raised an ear as I cocked the hammer on the gun, raised it left-handed around the edge of the bush, and pulled the trigger.

POP! It was a misfire. The cap went off, but not the charge. Of course that wasn't anything new with the old smoke pole. The same thing happened two years ago, when I'd also fired at a deer not 20 yards away.

The buck? Well, that noise didn't even put him to flight. He merely looked up, cast those big brown eyes my way, and returned to chomping on the grass.

It was somewhat disappointing from a hunter's standpoint, but I had more caps in my shoulder bag. I carefully began to unzip the bag, and that did the trick—he looked up at me once more, raised his tail, then slowly trotted off through the brush.

Darkness had settled in as I retraced my steps down the trail to the truck. I guess, again from a hunter's standpoint, I should have felt disappointed over the incident. But somehow I didn't feel anything of the sort. The deer was still alive and well to roam about another day—perhaps his offspring would do so for another century, or even a millennium.

And yes, I was thinking that although several centuries removed, William Shakespeare was indeed correct.

The chase will really be the thing. In this century, during a millennium, and perhaps even those to follow.

Interesting Deer Hunt with "Dumb Old Gerald"

I 've fished several times with an old buddy I used to refer to as 'dumb old Gerald.' Well, we've also hunted together for rabbits, squirrels and even deer. And I must say that although Gerald was and is an expert fisherman, he originally lacked any knowledge of deer hunting.

The first and only time we hunted deer together was an experience for the books. Actually, it made me want to tie his shoelaces together and throw him out the cabin door into the swamp.

Let's return to that thrilling day of yesteryear.

Gerald was a different sort of 'bloke,' and did I mention that he was a transplant from Australia? Well, he was, and he moved to Michigan with his parents from along an outback billabong when he was eleven. And since he'd already taken on the 'burl of spakin' Australian,' was sometimes, no, always, next to impossible to understand.

For a time Gerald and I attended the same school, and that was when I was learning to become a hunter and fisherman, which I was to discover he already was!

Our first hunting adventure as 'mates' just happened to be a November deer hunt. Well, Gerald jumped in the car with dad and me at six in the morning, waving about a new 12-gauge shotgun his father had purchased for him the day before. Dad gave me one of those

I-told-you-so looks as he rapidly removed the gun from Gerald's grasp and stuffed it in the trunk with ours.

"Well," beamed Gerald, "Let's 'ave a go at them roos!"

"Roos?" says I, shooting him a look of disbelief. "We're not after any hopping kangaroos. Deer's what we're after."

"Hang on a tick," he replied. "What's a deer?"

I glanced at my father, who was suddenly slouched down behind the wheel with a look of impending peril on his face. So, with an inkling of an approaching disaster and a sudden view of my father tossing Gerald from a moving vehicle, I jerked my head around and faced the rear seat.

"Deer! You know. You've seen pictures of 'em in school—those animals with flashing white tails, and sometimes even with antlers!"

"Well Bob's your uncle," said a wide-eyed Gerald, "I got it. We've some of them down under too. Still, probably like huntin' roos. Guess I was away with the pixies for a tick. So deer are the dinkum we're about. Well stone the crows!"

At that point I turned back to pretend to actually notice the woods along the two-track road, thinking a nightmare was approaching.

"You boys better hunt near me this morning," dad finally remarked with a glance in my direction. "It'll be safer for all of us that way."

It was a typical, freezing November morning with a light snow falling when dad finally parked the car and ferreted around in the trunk for our guns and ammo. His was a 30/06 and mine a single-barrel 12-gauge similar to Gerald's. I was handed a box of slugs and turned to ask Gerald where his were.

"Well guts for garters," he exclaimed, "I'm a boofhead if I didn't leave 'em back in the dunny!"

I wasn't certain what a 'dunny' was at the time, but hastened to dig into my own shells and hand him a few.

'Don't load those guns until we're up the trail and into position," cautioned dad as we hiked into the woods a ways. Then he pointed me over to a stump and said, ""I'll take Gerald on in some and then return to where I'm between you guys." And just then I thought I caught a moment of hesitation, as though he'd had a sudden revelation of placing himself in a crossfire. Then they continued up the trail.

Anyway, I sat down on that stump and waited for daylight. It was a quiet morning thus far, and gradually getting light enough to see deer, perhaps even antlers.

A brief snow shower had somewhat ebbed when a shot rang out to my right, fairly close by. Then I heard hooves pounding in my direction and looked to see a buck with a large rack bounding right at me! And, almost unbelievably, the buck stopped about 20 yards away and turned sideways, sniffing the air.

I raised my shotgun, aimed and fired, and rather than a loud report and a slam to my shoulder, there came a subtle 'click'—I'd given Gerald some shells and forgot to load my own gun!

Of course the deer heard that click, glanced my way, and escaped at an angle to my left.

Dad was suddenly at my side. "Was that you that fired? Did you get 'im?"

I then explained what I'd done, or foolishly not done, all coming out as dad stood there in disbelief.

And just then another shot rang out from up the hill. We looked at each other with no little amazement.

"Has to be Gerald," was all I said.

So we hurried up the hill to find 'dumb old Gerald' hovering over 'my' eight-point buck, and 'flash as a rat' there he was, decked out in rapture and a huge smile.

"Man," he says, 'that roo was comin' at me flat out like a lizard drinkin—put the wind up me for a tick! But I got 'im."

So 'dumb old Gerald' had really done it. Never mind that he didn't know a deer from a roo, or that he'd forgotten his own shells. We congratulated him anyway.

After all, dad and I were only a couple of 'septic tanks' (Americans, if you will) while 'dumb old Gerald' was a natural-born hunter, a 'tall poppy' from way down under!

A Deer Season opener to forget.

The Rules of Hunting—I Think

Sure, the deer hunting seasons may be over for now, but so many deer hunters are still telling about their experiences during the various seasons that I feel compelled to hatch up one more account of my own.

And deer hunting has certainly changed. For one thing it has become a very 'antlered' event.

Remember the good old days when we'd just go hunting and weren't concerned about a myriad of new laws and regulation changes? Life was much easier then. We didn't really worry much about the area we were tromping through, whether to shoot a buck or a doe or one of each, the number and length of antler points on the animal's starboard side, or even hunting by the dark of the moon.

Well now, I've been giving some of the newer regulations some thought and even a little concentration, and I believe I know what's happened.

It's a conspiracy!

Yep, whenever the DNR finds their coffers running low, or perhaps their need to raise salaries a bundle, it goes on a new-law and regulation feeding frenzy. And such new or adjusted stuff is guaranteed to get the average hunter arrested at will and hit with a magnificent fine. Ah, the DNR's piggy bank is full again!

Now, I don't know about you, but I know I'm not a graduate of M.I.T., and I don't drag a Ha'vard lawyer around with me on hunting trips.

"But Ed," you may say, just as my brother Ross did up at camp and just prior to deer season, "you're an outdoor writer. Surely you must know all these new regulations."

"My name's not Shirley and I don't know all that stuff," I grunted back.

"At least you can tell me how many deer I can shoot, can't you," he entreated.

Here he was, on one of his 'bent-for-election' trips, so I decided to humor the rascal with my recently-found expanse of outdoor knowledge.

"Well first, it depends upon where you're hunting and how many licenses you can purchase. You could buy one firearm license and one archery license, or even a combination license with two kill tags."

"That's a simple enough thing. So I can get two deer, right?"

"If you're lucky," I answered, scowling down at my old swampers. "But sometimes it isn't that simple. Sometimes during the archery season you can get several antlerless deer, or even two antlered bucks. But at least one of those bucks must have four or more antler points on one side. Or sometimes you can get one antlerless deer and one antlered buck. Clear enough, eh?"

Ross scratched his head as a sudden realization hit him. "Oh ya," he scowled, "I can just picture me running down a deer with my counter and tape measure...Here deer, here deer. Get yourself over here so I can count and attempt to measure those antler points before I shoot you!"

"Not to worry," I countered. "Think of all the good things the DNR can do with the loot from your fine."

"I just did, and I don't particularly like the idea. Besides, this 'antlered' and 'antlerless' thing still has me confused."

At that point I reached for a glass of water and a couple of Alka-Seltzer before replying, "'Antlered' means a deer with at least one antler three inches long. 'Antlerless' means one without antlers, or could even be one with antlers less than three inches long."

Ross walked over to the fridge and retrieved a can of something that hissed when he opened it. "Well," he queried. "Is that it? It's just that simple, eh?"

"Wait, there's more," I said. "In some areas the season bag limit for antlered bucks may be two."

"So, is that all?"

"Hardly," I replied, beginning to really enjoy this as I emptied my glass of Alka-Seltzer. "During the firearms and muzzle loading seasons you can shoot two antlered bucks, one of which must..."

"I know! I know! Have longer antlers...I believe I'm going to be sick."

"At least we've had an excellent past year," I sighed. "All those acorns and other nuts will be good for antler growth."

"Nuts is right! Enough all ready!"

"No, there's still more," I smiled at him. "There's the private, state and federal land issues..."

"That's enough!" Ross proclaimed, tossing his hunting guide booklet on the poker table. "I'm going fishing instead!"

"Be careful," I sez. The fishing season is now closed in some areas, curtailed in others, and the size limits on some species has changed..."

There was no reply. Only a deafening and ominous silence.

A Small Game 'Animal Court'

I was in a hunting area I knew well and on the opening day of small game season I took about a three-mile hike through the woods, skirting the edge of a swamp through the pine and oak trees and across the uplands.

I'd had success there before. This time the hunting was good too. I managed to harvest a grouse and a couple squirrels during the first half of the hike, which would eventually take me on a roundabout route back to the truck.

But it was different this year. My usual hunting pard, Chuck, was working that day and I no longer had my old-fashioned "feather-finder" dog Chipper for companionship. I suppose I was actually feeling a little on the lonely side or melancholy.

It was a blustery day, raining cats and dogs one minute and the sun flashing rainbows through the trees the next. Suddenly, I spotted what appeared at first glance to be a hornet nest in a wind-blown tree up ahead, but on closer inspection the gray ball began to move and expand its needles. It was a very large porcupine.

Now I suppose we sometimes do some rather childish things, so I called out, "Hey, you, watcha doin' up there?" Well, the porky looked down on me, then gnashed its teeth and stomped a front foot several times. Then it slowly worked its way up the old oak tree.

It was about midday in my route and I was feeling somewhat leg-weary, so I stopped and sat down with my back against the porky's oak tree, my shotgun across my knees. The warm sun was now splashing through the leaves above and I slowly began to feel rested. Then drowsiness overcame me and I snoozed.

"Order in the court!" snapped someone, striking a gavel, and I looked up to see Mr. Porcupine seated as a judge, gavel in hand and peering nastily down at me through dark-rimmed glasses.

"These proceedings are under way," he announced sternly. "And I want first to hear from the defendant, Mr. Hunter. Well, what do you have to say for yourself?"

I was stricken with a sudden feeling that I wasn't in Kansas anymore, or Michigan, or anywhere else I was familiar with. I glanced hurriedly around an animal-filled courtroom, then to the jury box where sat six squirrels, three grouse and three rabbits, each one chattering or squawking and giving me the thumbs-down signal.

"Hang 'im!" they yelled out in unison.

"Well?" the porky judge repeated. "Speak up!" Then peering around the courtroom, he shouted, "Order here, or else I'll shoot some of you myself!"

I was nonplused by his wit. "Shoot some of you myself" coming for a judge? This had to be some sort of nightmare or else my flux-capacitor had malfunctioned and I'd been shot into hyperspace. At best, I was no longer on the quiet hike through the woods.

"Wha … what are the … charges? Why am I here? " I finally stammered.

"Charges? Charges?" snapped the porky. "Why, you have two squirrels and a partridge in your pear-shaped game vest right now! What do you suppose you're being charged with, a breaking and entering?"

I suddenly knew that I was trapped and if I didn't come up with something soon this guy would prove he was indeed a hanging judge.

"Well, judge," I says, finally getting some wits about me. "You know that each year about this time we in Michigan have what we call a small game season, and if we purchase a license we humans are allowed to hunt some of you…"

"Hang 'im!" yelled the gallery of jurors in unison once more.

"Now hold on a minute," I countered. "You animals have your pecking order as you call it. So do we. After all, God gave humans domination over you, so I'm within my given rights. Besides, most of us hunters can't hit the broad side of a barn anyway. I know I can't. I was just lucky this morning, that's all."

"Hang 'im!" yelled the jury again.

I now was convinced that this thing was out of hand and if something didn't alter their thinking, I'd soon be hanging by a yellow ribbon 'round the old oak tree.

Ah, but something did happen. Suddenly I heard loud barking and my dog, Chipper, came charging into the courtroom. To wit, the animals, including the judge, scattered to the winds and evaporated.

I awoke to find my hunting partner's dog, Quincy, not my Chipper, licking my face. Chuck had made it up to hunt after all.

"Maybe it's a good thing we did come, at that," Chuck interrupted, as he glanced upward over my head.

"That big porky about six feet over your head looks as though he's about to land on you and chew off one of your ears!"

Well, we left the judge, er, porky, and hunted our way back to our vehicles. I never actually told Chuck about my "animal court" nightmare, but I sure as heck wasn't about to take any more shots at animals that opening day.

Several Ways to 'Bark' at Squirrels

E veryone has 'barked' up the wrong tree at sometime or other. You know, wrongly accused someone, said something later regretted, or made a mistake here and there.

Well now, I say that if you're wanting to 'bark' at something, go squirrel hunting.

Squirrels do bark, although it's more like a put-put-putting sound, and they do so when they see or hear what they consider to be danger approaching. It's done to warn their species that something unusual is a'foot, and that could be you, the hunter.

But, should a hunter himself, or herself, do a little 'barking' of their own, a squirrel may indeed answer. Now, most squirrel hunters know that you don't go tromping noisily through the woods while after those little rodents. No, one walks carefully along and as soundlessly as possible, stopping often to survey the area ahead. Or, even find likely squirrel territory and sit down to wait.

Either way works, but I've found that in either case a little 'barking' of my own often leads to success. And it's an easy thing to do—just put your lips together tightly and make a put-put-put sound. Then wait for a squirrel to either answer or pass the word along. If one answers your call, just stay still and wait. They're curious little critters and will often come looking to see what's up.

There's yet another method and it's also often referred to as 'barking' a squirrel. It's really an aiming technique. While hiding along a tree trunk or a limb, a squirrel will usually lie flat and still, thinking it is hidden from your view. However, if you can see a little of it, excluding the tail of course, a carefully placed shot just below it on the tree bark itself can do the trick. Try it, it works.

Of course all of the above precludes hunting with a dog that is accustomed to chasing and treeing squirrels. I only had one I could actually call a squirrel dog. His name was Rowdy and he'd somehow learned a great trick. When a squirrel was treed, I'd remain on one side of the tree and he'd move to the other side and create a ruckus. This caused the critter to move into view on my side of the limb where I could get a good shot.

Still, with all the put-putting and limb barking, I much prefer to hike into squirrel territory and sit down with a good magazine or book. Then to just wait for one to show up. Yes, the opposite may be true if I still had ol' squirrel-chasin' Rowdy, but he's chasin' 'em elsewhere now.

So squirrel season may now be open, along with the grouse, woodcock and rabbit seasons. That encompasses a lot of hunting, particularly should one go after all four game species. But even if you are a multiple hunter, try pulling up a stump once in a while and do a little put-put-putting. Try it and you too could be rewarded with some tasty table fare…And should a crow answer your call, put him away too as crow season may also be on. But a warning: I wouldn't recommend a crow as table fare!

This is not a good thing!

A 'Deer Hunting Reality' Show

Maybe those television reality shows are not so far out as some of us think they are.

Could be their reason for being so popular is that so many of us have been in Fantasy Land or Never-Never Land for so long we're yearning to get back to some reality in life—albeit a strange way to do it.

Not! Well, at least not this guy.

However, I do have a glimmer of an idea for a new and unique reality show, one that could really pop some eye balls and even send a TV station's ratings skyrocketing. I saw it in a dream.

I call it "Deer Hunting Reality."

First, we search out 10 wannabe deer hunters from downtown New York City. We pick five ladies and five guys, none of whom has ever seen a deer rifle, let alone a deer.

Next, we transport them to a wooded section of land in northern Michigan. There, we station five guy "drivers" heading east and five gal "sitters" looking back west, say about a thousand yards apart.

Now we hand each a rifle and some ammunition, all the while bearing in mind that not one of them has the faintest idea how to load, aim and fire a rifle.

Cruel, you say? Na. Remember, this is a reality show and those always contain a goodly element of danger along with the unexpected.

Of course, the objective is to harvest (dare I say kill?) a deer. The first one to do so wins a million dollars.

But ah, the consequences. Anyone injuring or killing another person, or themselves, is immediately ejected from the show, arrested and thrown into jail. Again, cruel? No. Remember this is the ultimate reality experience, where not only getting a deer is the goal but, just perhaps, survival is of even more importance.

Finally, we station two cameramen, or camerawomen, with each line. Those with the drivers will follow along with them and the two with the sitters will spread out, dig a hole and hunker down to avoid the passage of a bullet.

Now we set a starting time as well as a time limit of say, 30 minutes, and turn the drivers loose. They spread out at intervals of 100 feet or so and enter the woods.

As a final reality, we have actually chosen an area frequented by many deer—hard to come by in northern Michigan in recent years. But behold, deer are suddenly on the move.

Cameras roll as deer begin to flee. Shots are fired and shouts echo through the woods.

"Hey! Why are you shooting at me?"

"I think I got a piece of one!"

"Someone show me how to load this thing, will you?"

"My gun won't work."

"I think I hit one. Oh, sorry, Martha. Was that you?"

The drivers finally close in on the sitters and the scene is utter bedlam and confusion.

"Wow! Did you see all those deer?"

"Yeah. I shot at least a 10-point something or other. Well, I think it was a deer."

"Boy, those three female deer went by me like jets. I didn't even get a shot."

"Hey, I still can't load this thingy!"

"I stumbled over a log and this gun went off. Do they always do that?"

At last the director herds the hunters together and asks if anyone got a deer. No one answers in the affirmative.

"Well," the director laughs. "I'll tell you why. It's the surprise. You see, none of you could have actually shot a deer, or anything else for that matter. Everyone was given blank ammunition. The idea was to give you a taste of what could happen on a real deer hunt. Exciting, wasn't it?"

"Sure, but no one gets the million bucks," someone complains.

"That's a fact," the director says. "However, each of you will receive 100,000 big ones for taking part in this, 'The Ultimate Hunting Reality Show.' Cheers. Everyone's happy. Fade to black."

Now, I regret to inform you that some of this similar, 'canned hunting' is actually going on now. Mostly it's for small game, however.

And now a little personal note from this writer. If any TV director or individual picks up on this idea and uses it for a show to hunt anything, without my written permission, I will sue the pants off him or her. And guess what? I'll get the million dollars.

The Crowning of King
in Whahoppen Forest

I t was election time in Whahoppen Forest, when its many inhabitants
would be voting to determine who would be pronounced King of
the Forest for the coming year.

Two whitetail stags were the obvious front runners—there was
"Bushy," who championed more animal freedom and declared that there
was really no need for larger government, and "Algie," who spoke for a
larger government and more restrictions on the forest kingdom. Bushy
was running on the "Freedom Party" ticket and Algie on the "Anything
Goes" ticket. Both had found "ho-hum" running mates that would
have little, if any, affect on the voters.

These worthies were challenged by a bear, who was running on the
"Stock Market" ticket, along with an old fox who declared himself to be
an "Independent". Neither expected to get many votes, but both were
power hungry and coveted the attention as well.

It was a lengthy campaign during which the major contenders ran
about the forest championing their causes. And it was sometimes a
bitter campaign, with each party accusing the other of wrongdoing and
indiscretions. Nearing election day, both were weary in mind and body,
having nearly lost their ability to speak, or even think, coherently.

But election day finally arrived, and the animals lined up at their
precinct trees (can't call 'em poles here) to place their votes. There were
deer, bear, fox, squirrel, owls and other birds and animals hurrying

to get in line. Of course, there was also some confusion as the rabbits always have a wary eye on the foxes, the deer were extremely nervous when near wolves and the bears were continually pushing their way to the forefront of the voting lines, causing the wrath of others. There were 100 precinct trees located throughout Whahoppen Forest. Some had simplified voting methods such as licking a stamp and placing it by either a picture of Bushy or one of Algie, while others needed a hole either stomped or chewed out beside the voter's choice.

But this became confusing at some of the trees, as many birds left scratches rather than actually pecking out holes, while other voters simply didn't or couldn't read or weren't amply prompted to place their stamp properly. Some became so disenchanted with their inability that they began to run about, challenging the validity of the election, demanding recounts, revote, and raising all sorts of doubts throughout the forest.

Ah, but it was finally time to close the trees and count the ballots, which in some instances were passed in front of the photo-memory-like eyes of the owls, while others were paw or peck counted individually.

Meanwhile, the two stags, Bushy and Algie, had retired to their forest glades to await the returns. But, when some election discrepancies began to be reported, both became concerned.

Early "exit" poles had shown that the election was too close to call, so each stag contacted his campaign manager, who immediately got in touch with their lawyers, tree workers and demonstrators, along with the lesser campaign workers.

This resulted in the filing of several lawsuits concerning the validity of elections at certain trees, and the local raccoon police squad was called to several precincts to confiscate some ballot boxes.

It was also reported that several boxes had also been either lost or misplaced. It was mayhem in the forest.

So, recounts began to occur within certain disputed precincts and continued again and again over six days—with Bushy and Algie trading leads, each time by a slim margin.

However, by Whahoppen Forest law, all ballots must be counted and a Forest King declared by the close of seven days.

And by the close of that sixth day, those in the Freedom Party and those within the Anything Goes Party were literally at each other's throats with extremists and outside agitators roaming the forest and causing all sorts of discontent within the ranks.

But on the morning of the seventh day, it happened! An idea struck Bushy and he loped over to Algie's glade to have a little talk.

"We've got to settle this thing," Bushy pronounced. "It's tearing our forest apart. And I have an idea. If we join forces, we can declare ourselves both winners, can rule side by side during this term—perhaps taking turns as King and Vice-King, so we can cover all the bases."

"That's not really Parliamentary procedure," Algie replied. "And I don't think it's even addressed in the Whahoppen Constitution. But you know, it just may be the answer."

"Well, we aren't always going to agree on things," said Bushy, "but that's what we have our Whahoppen Congress Committee for—and, while it may not please all of our constituent creatures out there, it just could bring the majority of them back together."

The two wise old stags agreed, clinked antlers on it, and headed out to inform the forest of their decision. The result was that the Whahoppen Congress, with a few abstentions, agreed to the co-King idea. It was adopted, and there was to be little confusion or anti-demonstrations to follow. There would be no bitterness in Whahoppen Forest.

That is, until the next election. And that would be when each of them would claim he could run as the incumbent.

In Love with My Old Winchester

I love my old Winchester Model 94, almost as much as I love the many dogs I've hunted with over the years. And, regardless of the fact that hunting season is over, unless one is out plinking predators, I'm going to write something about it today.

First, my advice is that if you do own one of those trusty old "Roy Rogers" specials, hang on to it. Even purchase one if you aren't lucky enough to own one.

Even though I'm aware that many 'gun experts' are not in accord with me on this, hunters and writers alike, some even scorning the Winchester .30-30 or even the Marlin variety, the .30-30 is the most widely distributed and used centerfire rifle in the United States. It has fired lead around this country for more than a century.

Here's where I part company with most outdoor writers, as many disdain this rifle in favor of the high-powered stuff. Most say this rifle cartridge doesn't shoot flat or hard enough, and they close their minds to it.

But the fact is that more .30-30 ammunition is sold yearly than any other cartridge—more than .30-06, the .270 or even the magnums.

Yeah, I know my old Winchester isn't a thing of beauty. Rather, it actually looks as thought it came off an old Roy Rogers movie set, as I've dinged it up considerably over these many years. But the gun simply works and continues to do its job.

One doesn't need to carry an 'elephant' gun in most areas of our state, as most deer are never shot at a distance of more than 100 yards, or say 200 yards at the maximum. And the bullet makes the difference. One can plink smaller game with the 125-grain bullet, then step up to 150-grain or more for larger game.

Thus, many Michigan hunters are found, like me, toting their old loose-lever .30-30 around the woods.

And another plus is that the carbine barrel is short. Sure, it decreases accuracy about 5 percent when compared to a 24-inch barrel or longer, but the short rifle is perfect when hunting in heavy cover or short range areas.

Still another advantage of my old .30-30 is that it's easier on the shoulder than the 'elephant' gun, and still may be fired in rapid succession.

Now, if we set aside all these little facts that many hunters don't care one hoot about, the Winchester 94 gives one more plus—it makes one really hunt. For myself, I seldom hunt where I need to glass or scope game, so it's more of a challenge to try to outsmart game rather than to cross-hair it at 400 yards.

OK, I admit that I could be stepping on some toes out there and that I have used the high-powered stuff as well. I'm merely saying that you could wipe the dust off that old .30-30 and try some trickery on game sometime. Perhaps crawl into some of our thick, forested areas and put a little hunting back into the hunt.

Perhaps a little personal account concerning the prowess of this rifle is in order.

I had returned to one of my favorite target-plinking areas up north and hiked about a half mile through the woods. When almost to an open field that contained stumps I intended to use for target practice, I suddenly heard thumping and brush-crashing noises behind me, along with some weird sounds that were somewhere between growls and bellows.

The sounds were closing in, and up the same trail I'd been on. Suddenly a huge buck with a nice rack leaped toward me from among the trees, so close I could almost smell its breath! He saw me and veered off, leaping and clearing a fallen tree by about 10 feet. I watched as he continued to crash onward in the wink of an eye.

Then along came the dog—just one, not a pack. But he was obviously bent on bringing down that deer.

Now, I don't use a scope on my .30-30, just open sights. Besides, a scope would really have been useless at this close range.

The dog was a large one, a mix of police-type mostly. He flashed into view and I snapped off a round, and when it hit him, he crashed down upon the fallen tree that moments before the buck had vaulted over.

Shooting any dog is distasteful to me, much as it is to many hunters. But most hunters will say that it is sometimes the proper thing to do—particularly if they are deer killers, as this one was. It obviously lived in the woods. It had no collar and was sinewy, with scars and marks around its body.

I didn't like it, but killing it was the thing to do. And I thought afterward that had it been deer season, I'd have been faced with quite a choice—to either shoot the deer or kill its would-be killer.

I still can't answer that, but I do know that my old .30-30 Winchester had once again done its job, and that that gun will be hanging around my house for a long time.

Five Days at Deer Camp...I Think

WEDNESDAY: Five of us arrived at deer camp this morning for five days of hunting, camaraderie and to much enjoy Michigan's outdoor wonderland. It was chilly, so we built a fire in the old woodstove. It's quite cozy now.

Tomorrow the season opens, so we played some poker and hit the sacks early. A light snow fell this afternoon, so tracking deer should be easy tomorrow. And the woods are simply beautiful.

I didn't win at poker today. My buddy Sam was the lucky one. Not to matter, this is just great!

THURSDAY: Awoke early and rekindled the stove. A thermometer that hangs on a tree outside a window reads 20 degrees, and nearly three inches of snow fell overnight. The trees are beautiful outside.

Left the cabin about five o'clock and hunted till 10. Saw a few deer, but no bucks. It gradually became colder and a heavy blanket of snow came down, so after going in for a brunch of bacon and eggs, I only hunted a few hours this afternoon. But it was sure great being in the outdoors. We played poker again this evening and I hardly won a hand, but my pal Sam was winning again. Boy, is he a lucky guy. We're all having a great time!

FRIDAY: Arose this morning to six more inches of snow, and the temperature hovered around 10 above zero. Trudged my way about half-a-mile to my deer stand and just got in position when the ice storm hit. It turned the tree limbs and branches into shimmering crystals—

nice to look at, but after several hours of icewater and snow running into my longjohns, and no deer sighted, I called it a day.

However, the other guys were up and had breakfast ready. Another six inches of snow arrived by nightfall and some of the guys were getting a little nervous. It's a good half mile down the old two-track to any road, and some fear that we may get snowed in.

Nobody hunted this afternoon. We just sat around, sort of getting on each other's nerves. I tried to remain calm and unconcerned. We played poker again, perhaps for four hours, and that lucky Sam seemed to win every other hand. I even wonder if he's cheating. But no, Sam wouldn't do that!

SATURDAY: Temperature around zero this morning. Nobody hunted. But some goofball left the damper open on the stove too long and we had a chimney fire. It was some time before we got the place warmed up again. Thought we may freeze to death. Went to the outhouse early and slipped on the steps, nearly breaking a leg. The other guys laughed. They're idiots!

Nearly two foot of the %*!# white stuff has fallen since our arrival here, and it's impossible to hunt. Mike tried to get his 4 by 4 out and made it about 50 feet before it hung up. Looks like we're here for the duration. I know all of us are pretending to remain calm, but tempers are flaring as the anxiety continues.

Played poker all afternoon and into the night. We fought over every hand, and Sam was the big winner. Again! I know the slob is cheating, but I can't prove it. But if he wins one hand tomorrow, I may kill him!

SUNDAY: Another eight inches of that !#*&* white stuff fell overnight. Looks as though the only way out will be to shovel a half-mile path, one step at a time. And there's only one shovel in the shed, an old manure shovel at that.

Why did I come to this rotten place anyway? There's no deer around here, and we may all die. I hate this white stuff!

Ah, I finally caught Sam cheating at the poker table, and I bent that old manure shovel over his stupid head! If I have to play one more hand of poker, I'm going to kill something! And guess what? It's turned even colder.

I know, I'll set fire to this stupid cabin tonight. That should warm things up!

A DAY LATER, I BELIEVE: I'm feeling fine just now. Must be those little pills the lady in the white dress forces down me every hour or so…But where am I, and why are these walls padded? Also, why am I strapped backwards in this white jacket??

Oh well, happy hunting to the rest of you!

Fun at Camp with Ross and Ed

My brother Ross and I were up at the cabin, sitting around and cleaning up some old hunting gear, when we sort of got on one of those nostalgic rolls.

We began to converse about some of the various experiences we'd had over the years, and since Ross is older I sort of let him carry the ball.

"You know, I hunted raccoons when I was a kid," Ross began, "then I'd make stretcher boards to put the hides on so they'd dry...Well, one summer an old hound dog wandered up to our farm house, and he turned out to be the best coon dog in the whole territory."

"How good was he?" I entreated, unwittingly walking right into Ross' trap.

"Good? He was so good that all I had to do was show him a stretcher board of any size and he'd run right out and find a raccoon to fit it!"

I laughed, thinking the story was over. It wasn't.

"Well, now," Ross continued, "one day that dog spotted mom's ironing board sittin' on the front porch and took off just a yippin. We never saw that dog again!"

"A likely story," I scoffed. Then I remembered that one time he'd trapped muskrat and mink while back in school, so thought I'd trap him this time. "Tell me, did you ever trap a skunk in one of your traps?"

"Well, I caught a mink once that was worth more money than Dad made in a week," came the reply as he obviously was trying to avoid the question.

"Mink, schmink," I said. "Did you ever catch a skunk in a trap?"

"Well, occasionally," came the reluctant reply. "I do remember one I caught. Dad and I were skinning it out in the barn, and we broke its sack by mistake. The sack, of course, was under pressure and we both got doused good. Ma wouldn't even let us in the house. She came out to the barn with pails of hot water and made us bathe there, twice. But you can hardly get that smell off you.

"I went to school the next morning and I guess I was pretty ripe, 'cause the teacher came over to me and whispered that maybe I should sit out in the hallway the rest of the week! Now, that was on Tuesday, and that evening Mom took another whiff of me and suggested that I pack a few things and take off hunting for three or four days…I did, and that's when I found the deer."

By then I was laughing so hard I nearly choked on a handful of peanuts I'd just chucked into my mouth.

"Deer?...What deer?"

Ross was really on a roll now. "Well," he sez, "it was my second day out in the woods, and smellin' like I did I figured I'd never get a shot. Then suddenly I cam across a button buck that had evidently tried to jump between two trees, came down in the middle and got wedged there. It looked like he'd been there a day or so, 'cause his sides were skinned up and he was plumb tired out. Anyway, I tried several hours to lift the deer out of there, and couldn't budge him. So I went to a nearby farmhouse where I asked two brothers, Buck and Garland Webster, if they'd give me a hand with the deer.

"The brothers owned an old Model-T truck, and we rattled it down through the woods. Finally, we couldn't get the truck any further, so we walked in and all lifted and pulled until the deer was free.

"That deer just stood there, so we petted it and talked to it, thinking it would eventually wander off. But it didn't, and each time we'd turn toward the truck, the deer followed along like a pet.

"Well, we finally got close enough to where that deer could see that old Model-T. He just looked at the "monster," but when one of the brothers started the rattle-trap up he took off h--l bent for election. So I guess it wasn't hurt much."

So story telling, for Ross, was about over. But I gave him a suspicious look as I said, "Now that last one sounded more like a true story than the others. They sounded a little fishy to me, and—,"

"They're all true, so help me!" he fired back, peering over his glasses. "Do you think I'd lie to you? What do you think I am, a 'heavy' or something?"

I had to smile back and laugh as I said, "Nah, youse'e ain't no heavy. Youse'e my brother!"

So I never did really get to carry the conversation much that evening. Ross did. And he was good at it…but my time will come. You'll see.

A Surprise Guest at the Cabin

I traveled up to the cabin one week night, and of course none of the other usual suspects were there. I decided it would be an excellent time to make some notes for forthcoming columns, so seated myself at the old poker table.

After writing for a while, I got up to open the cabin door to let in a little fresh air.

Then it happened. I had no idea where the large, old yellow-striped cat came from—out in the woods and lost, I thought. But I believe this one thought he'd suddenly found a home. He sprang through the door and immediately to the table, where he just sat and looked at me.

Well, I went back to my notes, and that old tom moved right in and began to scratch his head on my notebook. He was quite a large cat, and I admit that I did look for some little "bobs" in his ears. None were there, fortunately.

Now, I read somewhere that he who has a dog to worship him should have a cat to ignore him. Well, I've never been what one would call a cat lover. I've always accepted them around the house for the kid's sake and peace in the family. However, one place I've never liked to spot a cat is running loose in the woods. There they are a natural hunter and an enemy of small game.

Back to Old Tom. He was obviously scruffy, but looked as though he hadn't missed many meals. Must have weighed around 12 pounds or so. And between his purring and stepping all over me, I managed to finish my notes. Then I retrieved some leftovers from the refrigerator, and the cat charged right in and devoured every crumb.

"I guess that old stuff won't poison you," I remarked.

So I offered Tom some milk in an old cracked saucer. He lapped up every drop, pausing occasionally to glance up at me and purr as though offering a "thank you"

"Now, what am I going to do with you, Tom," I asked the cat and the cabin walls. "You certainly don't act wild, and could even be someone's pet. But it's a long jaunt to the nearest cabins or homes around here... Tell you what, in the morning we'll go for a ride and try to find your home."

That night I slept with old Tom curled at my ankles, and we ate breakfast together in the morning. Then I got the cat into the cab of my truck, finally. I've known cats that would take to a vehicle and some that would not—this one was the latter. He fought it, rendering me several scratches in the process.

But finally we were off, with Tom crouched in fright on the back of the passenger seat.

Well, stops at the first two cabins proved fruitless. At the first, a hunter informed me that the cat "looked wilder than a March hare," and it "would be a good idea to shoot it." Of course I resisted that idea and drove on to a second cabin, where no one was home.

About three miles farther on, we arrived at a year-round home where two young girls were playing in the yard. Now Tom got real excited and charged out as I opened the door.

The girls were now looking up and one squealed out, "Tinker Bell! It's really her!" She ran over and scooped up the cat, which made no resistance whatever.

Tinker Bell? Her?

Just then a guy with a stubble of beard stepped out the door and offered a hand. "Thanks," he said. "The kids thought she was gone forever. She's wandered off on occasion, but never for a week before this."

Then I explained that this time she'd "wandered" about four miles and that it may be best for the kids to keep a closer eye on their pet.

So I left, waving a fond farewell to my overnight companion. But again, Tinker Bell? Well, I hadn't looked to be certain. Besides, one may assume that male cats do more carousing about than do females... Still, it's a modern world, so who knows?

Lost on a Deer Hunt, and Found Again

When a deer hunter becomes lost in a 30-mile swamp, things can get quite frightening.

But sure, most deer hunters will never fess up to being lost in the woods, every one of us a Dan Boone! Well, allow me to relate an experience from our deer camp.

I had intended to carry a book along on the opening morning of archery season. It was a book written by Steve Chapman, entitled, "A Look at Life from a Deer Stand," and was given to me by the minister of my church. But I forgot the book and left it at camp, making the discovery after trudging about three-quarters of a mile to my stand.

It was one of those days when all you see is squirrels and other rodents scurrying around, but no deer. That first day I never even saw another hunter, but I knew the lay of the land and was certain I'd see deer the second day.

Yes, I knew the territory very well, but there was a new member in our camp who was unfamiliar with the area. His name is Bill, and he is young, full of adventure, but inexperienced. He'd arrived at camp with an older friend who did know his way about the woods, but who did a foolish thing on that second morning of hunting. (I was to find out the details later.) Knowing the youngster's impatience to move about rather than sit in a stand, he asked young Bill to complete a circle out and back through a swale, to perhaps drive a deer back in his direction. That had been about nine o'clock in the morning.

Meanwhile, I'd sat in my stand since about seven, about a mile from where Bill began his 'small' circle. This time I'd remembered to bring along that book, and about two o'clock in the afternoon was engrossed in reading when the snapping of a distant branch caught my attention. Ah, perhaps a deer. I put the book down in the crook of a tree limb and peered carefully about.

Then came another snap of a twig, and suddenly through the brush I saw something move. Then I saw that it wasn't a deer but a hunter, and he was moving straight toward the center of the swamp—and a 25-mile hike if he were to continue in that direction!

I let out a low whistle, somewhat akin to a bob white. The hunter stopped, appeared to listen for a moment, then continued onward. I whistled again, and this time he paused and whistled back. So I stood up, waved and yelled, "Over here!"

Upon seeing me, the hunter scrambled over logs and brush to get to where I was. Yes, it was young Bill, and he sure was excited and relieved to "find" me.

I asked the obvious, "Where were you going?"

The boy answered hesitantly, "Well, I was trying to make a deer drive for Scottie, but I guess I circled out too far and really go messed up. I didn't bring my compass along, either. Boy, they're sure going to have fun with me in camp tonight."

Now, about then I decided he'd already learned a big lesson. "I don't think so," I said. "We'll just tell 'em that you circled a bit too far out and ran into me, so we decided to hunt together a few hours. No real harm in that, is there?"

Bill's eyes lit up then and he looked up, smiling. "Thanks," he said. "Next time I'll come out more prepared."

So we headed back down the ridge trail and back to camp.

But that book I was reading? Guess I'll never finish the last few pages because the next day it was gone. But who knows, maybe another "lost" hunter found it along with my trail out. I certainly don't mind, particularly if that hunter passes the book on to another hunter.

A Retreat for 'The Birds'

Wife Gerri and I hadn't been north to the cabin for a while, so decided to go there for a quiet weekend. But as we drove the last half-mile down the two track through the snow, harrowing things started flashing through our minds.

Could someone possibly have broken in and trashed the place? Could there have been damage from a recent wind storm? Could it have burned to the ground? Maybe animals could have found their way in. Bears can go right through windows or walls if they really want to, and raccoons could find their way in through the smallest entrance, and can certainly cause a lot of damage in a short time.

After unlocking and opening the main gate, my first duty was to spread a little corn outside to perhaps draw in a few deer, turkeys or other critters for viewing. And we'd hardly unloaded our duffel and cooler when in came several deer, followed by five turkeys and two squirrels. Actually, they were hungry and paid little attention to us at all.

Watching the animals and birds from a window, my wife suddenly cried out, "Hey, there's a strange noise coming from the wood stove!" Well, there hadn't been a fire in it for several weeks, so I guessed anything was possible. And something was in the stove all right, and it was now flopping about and making all sorts of weird noises.

So, asking Gerri to open wide all three cabin doors, I carefully swung open the stove door.

Well, with the most awful screeching possible, a raven popped out of the stove and onto the floor. Then, after flying up and bouncing off several windows and walls, it flew out the main door. But as it made its exit, I'll swear the raven was screeching out, "Nevermore! Nevermore!" (With due credit to that famous bard, Edgar Allen Poe.)

But actually, it was difficult to tell which was screeching the loudest, the raven or my wife!

Following that little experience, we got a warm fire going in the old stove and decided to take a little hike through the woods. There is a swamp nearby, and a little water that was not yet turned to ice proved to be a haven for a few ducks. We stood nearby and watched, and they didn't seem to mind our being there at all. I know I shouldn't have, but finally I let go with a "squaak" and off they went—southward, I hope.

On the way back to the cabin a young deer suddenly appeared before us. There were no other deer in sight, so we decided to approach it. Then a "whoof" came from the nearby brush and off it dashed.

That evening we heard a strange, yet somehow familiar sound outside. We went out to investigate. Now, where it came from I have no idea, but there, nearly in the top of a nearby pine tree, sat a large, yellow cat. We tried to call it down, but to no avail.

The tree was slender but tall, quite unclimbable. So I came up with a brilliant idea! I retrieved a rope from the truck and tied one end of it as far up the tree as I could reach, and the other end to the rear bumper of the truck. Maybe I could pull the tree over far enough so one of us could reach the cat.

Well, things were going just great as I eased the truck forward to where one of us could almost reach the animal. Then "sproong" as the rope broke, sending the tree upward and the cat off through the air! It may have put it in orbit, as we saw neither hide nor hair of the feline after that!

You know, thinking back at that experience, it may have been a good thing not to have reached that cat. I believe it had a bobbed tail.

The last morning of our retreat we took a ride around the area's roads and two tracks, and where, during the fall turkey season we'd seen hardly any strutters or hens, now we nearly had to shoo them off the roads. Funny how that works, isn't it?

Gerri and I retreat to the cabin sometimes to go hunting or fishing, even if such occasionally turns out to be for the birds or the animals that frequent the area, as this trip did. We'll keep returning, not like the raven's "Nevermore! Nevermore!"

Deer Huntin' wit da Svampers

Wit da firearms deer season just a day avay, I find myself in an upen ze backen den lookin' quandary. No, it isn't dat I'm not lookin' forward to da deer huntin'. I sure am. But I guess I'll just have ta admit dat rather than da huntin' it's da hunters dat concern me da most. An' more specifically, da bunch of svampers I hunt wit.

So, rather dan lookin' ahead, I'm lookin' ze backen!

About ten of us annually fill up da kabin near da Baldwin/Luther Svamp for da first veek of da season. And say, by golley, I'm really vondering if I can co-exist with dose animals through anuder opening veek.

Most of da huntin' party (yes, for some of dem it is a party) is made up of characters I've long ago svorn to avoid all-togeder. Guess I'd never associate with dem udervise.

Perhaps I'll give you a little rundown—an perhaps dat's da very word dey deserve—on a few of dem revolutionaries. Den you can be da judge.

"Mr. Clean," when he's not at da poker table, is constantly cleaning his rifle. I don't know vy dat is, 'cause he never hunts. An' perhaps da name Mr. Clean is an exaggeration too, because I tink his red flannel longjohns could stand up in da corner all by demselves after da fort day at da camp!

"Da Leader," is anuder vunce-in-da-vile hunter. An' perhaps ve should have dubbed him "Da Youper," cause he's extremely musically

155

declined an' drums on da voodstove vile fiddling wit his moustache all da time. Dat's very disturbing ven von is tryin' to sleep off da night before. Know vat I mean?

Now "Cookie," he doesn't go out to da huntin', aldough he still braggs about da eight-point he shot true da winder four years ago. No von complains about his cookin' dough, even dough all ve ever have is da chilli an' da beans. You hunters know vat I mean by dat, too.

An' den der's "Trash." Now he's da real hunter an' outdoosman of kamp. However, ve call 'em Trash 'cause he's alvays pickin' up da loose stuff around da area. Den he takes it out to burn in da firepit. Maybe he's a firebug, I don't know, but I do know he's a great shot wit his thunderboomer—gets a deer each year before anyone else.

Now, you take da "Retread"—please! he's da real character, and von dat I'd like ta see take up residence in a cave full of da bears. He's alvays tearin' down da two-track into da town with his beat up ol' Shoveitorleaveit, vile firin' his .45 pistola out da vender an' into da air. Says he's goin' for supplies, but alvays returns wit more of da Budviser. Fortunately, Retread don't hunt much. He'd need to sober up virst, an' I tink he's under da alkafluence of inkahol most of da time. Ve all hope a conversation officer gets 'em sometime!

Yet anuder individual in camp constantly pleads for a game of da poker. Don't really know vy he does dat, cause he bluffs constantly an' never vins a hand. His real name is Bill, but ve call 'em "Slick Villie" 'cause he tries to cheat all da time. Vell, Villie does hunt vunce or tvice during da veek, but I can't remember him ever takin' no venison to da home. If he does, he probably buys it on da vay soute.

Vell, perhaps now you can realize my quandary, if dat's da right vord. Sometimes I feel like I'm da only one in da kamp dat's sane.

But what da heck, I'll go again dis year. An' I like ta have some fun too, an' I really like da huntin' deer. I'll just have ta make up my mind dat dis year I'm not going ta let any of doze guys effect me…effect me…effect me…

Snapping Deer Photos at Night

Even though you may have spent a great deal of time in an area you've hunted, things can be totally different in that same area at night.

Things can actually be a little scary.

I had my camera along and was sitting quietly one evening, waiting for any sound of animal movement. Suddenly an owl began to hoot, setting off a chain reaction by coyotes in the area and making my blood run a little cold.

The clouds had erased any available light moments before, and the illumination from my watch and the camera screen were little comfort.

I was nestled down in a hole behind a long, an area I'd hunted many times before. But that was during daylight, not in the pitch blackness.

A few more coyotes yipped, then came a musical chorus from a nearby pack. And they were close, maybe right in front of me, or so I thought. Then I realized they were moving up a trail that led right to me, so I rested my camera on my knee, aiming it slightly toward the trail and along a rocky ledge.

Yes, right then I was beginning to wonder if coming out here hadn't been a bit on the foolish side, but moving now would be too late.

Then the leader of the pack stopped, and I could hear him sniffing the air, perhaps trying to single me out. He was directly in front of me, and my heart did a couple of flips. Will he attack? If so, it's certain the rest of the pack will follow. I could be in big trouble here.

Then the leader of the pack jumped to the side, up and over some brush, and the rest of the pack followed. They hardly made a sound as I snapped the shutter on my camera and the brief flash that followed gave me a glimpse of the fleeing animals. Then they were gone.

I settled back into the hole and wondered if I should get out of there while the getting was good. But my dendrites were returning to normal then, and I started to rationalize...I knew these woods. Hunted 'em many times, although then I'd had either a gun or bow along. Only difference now is the pitch blackness.

So I decided to stay put for the moment. However, should those coyotes return, what then?

Then came a different sound down that same path the coyotes had been on. It was the sound of hooves. Deer? Yes, but not small deer. These were large animals and the sound was quite unlike that made by deer I'd seen in this area before.

Suddenly, came the unexpected. The moon peaked out from behind the clouds for a few seconds, and before me stood two of the largest whitetails I've ever seen—deer with those "antlers like a liar" we always talk about at deer camp, but no one seems to harvest.

I almost had time to wonder where these guys go during deer season, but then realized I had to get my camera up and take a snap. The first deer hasn't moved, but the second one bolted up and off to the side as I took the shot. Then they were gone, and darkness returned to the woods.

I'll admit I was a little shaky as I ferreted out my flashlight and worked my way back to the cabin. And I knew what awaited me at the cabin. If I related such a wild story about monster whitetails someone would surely say, "Oh yeah? Remember the photo of that big black bear you almost got last spring? Yaddada, yaddada..."

So I'd simply tell 'em to wait for the proof...They'll see.

A Paper Plate, a Deer, and a Crossbow

I often climb up on the cabin roof to practice shooting my bow downward at an angle. The target I use is usually a paper plate, placed upon a bale of hay.

I've subsequently adjusted my shooting to accommodate the height and angle factor. That is, not hitting over or under the target, which easily occurs when shooting a bow at a downward angle.

But you know, all such practice still has me in a quandary. You see, having struck the target many times, I've yet to see a deer in the woods with a paper plate appearing over its vitals!

Maybe such is the answer to why I seldom get a deer with a bow. Surely there's no other reason! And most certainly it can't be that I get too excited and don't take time to aim and make a proper release. Na, can't be that.

Ah, perhaps I should try a crossbow. However, those, although one believes they can aim and shoot as though holding a rifle or shotgun, require a reasonable amount of practice.

Perhaps I should explain…Several seasons ago, one of our hunting group purchased a crossbow and brought it to our camp. He had proper authority to use the bow, but said he hadn't practiced much.

So on the afternoon prior to the bow season opener he set up a target and began to fire away. Fact is, all of us got into the act as none in our hunting party had any previous experience with the weapon. Well, we did pretty good for beginners, but noticed that the bow's owner wasn't doing so well. He'd hit the paper plate on occasion, but most of his hits sprayed around it—way around it!

One brave soul in camp had the nerve to suggest that the hunter not use the crossbow but return to his compound for the following morning's opener. Saying it may be best if he did so until he had more practice with his new weapon.

"Hey, I just paid six hundred dollars for this thing," the guy fired back, "and I'm gonna' hunt with it tomorrow. You'll see. I'll do just fine."

I almost hesitate to tell you what happened the following morning. But in the interest of proper deer hunting itself, I'll do so.

Each in our hunting party had separate tree stands, and each took to his stand prior to daylight with the understanding that around 10 o'clock we'd all return to the cabin for a late breakfast.

Upon our return the stories ran rampant.

"I had three deer right below me and couldn't move for a good shot."

"My string caught in my head net when I released, and the arrow stuck into a tree about 30 feet up."

And on and on it went, with no real success—until along came our crossbow hunter.

"I hit three deer this morning," he said sadly. "None of 'em dropped and I couldn't find any of 'em."

Our jaws nearly hit our boots as we all looked at him in disbelief.

"Did you hit any vital areas?"

"Did you find any blood trails?"

"How long did you look?"

"In what direction from your stand did they run?"

Perhaps needless to say, at that point breakfast was called off and everyone returned to his stand area, where we spread out looking for either a downed deer or any blood. Neither was found after several hours of scouring the woods in all directions.

Now then, I'll allow that the fellow felt bad enough about what he'd done. But if he'd hit a deer at all, it most certainly wasn't in any vital area for a kill—at least not for an immediate kill. And that wasn't something the rest of us could appreciate.

That particular hunter has not been invited back to our camp since, and yeah, I know that's tough. But deer hunting has its ethics, as does any form of hunting. And a crossbow hunter needs to practice as anyone else has to do, to be sure of a good hit—yes, on a paper plate, but especially for when he gets the opportunity to shoot at the real thing.

The Legend of "Old Big Foot" Solved

According to a news brief, a 3-point buck entered a Family Fare store near Grand Rapids one time.

It was reported that the deer slipped inside when someone activated an automatic door, and the buck worked its way toward a pet food aisle, finally toward a display of doughnuts.

I'd say it was quite likely that the deer was hungry but was torn between chowing down on pet food or ravaging those wafting doughnuts.

Ah, but the buck never had a chance to eat, as a couple of workers took hold of it by its antlers and escorted it outside.

Now, unless this news release was some sort of Halloween prank, fabricated as some writers tend to do (not me, ever!), I'd conclude that this poor deer was discriminated against and should immediately gather up some lawyers.

No question about it, the deer was not allowed access to any forage but was forced out of the building. And after all, who knows, the buck may have had a few bucks of its own and been able to pay up, one way or another. Well, don't we have many lawsuits much more frivolous today than in this case?

So, should someone be able to track down this deer, that is before it gets shot or otherwise arrested by a hunter, they should contact a lawyer or two and be prepared to explain certain rights to it.

I believe that this deer has a good case and could win a few sacks of food or doughnuts...Then again, maybe not.

Now such was an actual news brief. Would I lie to you? And if it were a fabrication, wouldn't that 3-point buck have been depicted as a 10-point, or even a 12-pointer?

You betcha!

However, most stories about seeing bucks with "antlers like a liar" don't come out of supermarkets, or even their tabloids. No, they come from the woods and from us who hunt those Michigan whitetails.

For example, for some years many members of our hunting party have been after a huge buck we named "Old Big Foot." It was rarely seen, and then only in flashes as it escaped our gun sights.

The deer came near the cabin on occasion, but always seemed to remain with its huge antler spread blending with the brush and trees. But there was no question as to its existence, as many times we discovered its huge tracks, and they were more the size an elk would make.

With the passing years Old Big Foot became somewhat of a legend. That is until a recent hunting season when I was awakened in the early morning by a noise outside the cabin. Then, sneaking outside, I discovered the secret of Old Big Foot.

For there, walking carefully along and stomping something into the ground was Sid, an older member of our group. Sid had shaped and nailed together a huge wooden hoof, and was going about his deceitful task.

Well, old Sid knew he was caught, but explained that the legend of Old Big Foot must continue on, not so much for us older guys, but for the thrill and enjoyment of the younger generation in camp.

Then Sid did a strange thing. He handed me the hoof he'd fashioned, saying, "Here, it's time someone else took this responsibility. So it's yours now. And remember, you need to keep the spirit of Old Big Foot alive, and to never tell anyone until it's time to pass the secret on."

Good old Sid has since gone to the "Happy Hunting Grounds," but I can tell you that on a late evening or early morning around our hunting area, one can still hear Old Big Foot as he stomps his way around the cabin and through the forest.

A Strange Way to Kill a Deer

I receive mail from some who question some of the columns I write about hunting or fishing. No, it's not that they don't enjoy them, it's more akin to "Did that really happen to you?" Or even, "Wow! That was way out!"

Well, let me say that such remarks don't bother me in the least, because actual occurrences are often more questioning than anything our imaginations can conjure up.

All of us are aware that there are literally zillions of tales about hunting camps and deer hunting, and I was witness to one such "impossible" event a few seasons ago at our deer camp.

Allow me to set the stage for you and relate this one. And yes, this one was indeed "way out!"

I was situated comfortably in one of our deer blinds awaiting almost anything with antlers to come picking its way along when a shot rang out about 100 yards down the ridge from me. It sounded like George's .30-.30 Winchester. Now, George is one of my hunting buddies, and I knew the location of his stand as well as the rifle he toted.

Putting myself on full alert, I watched the downward trail intently. Then a second shot rang out, and this one was closer to me. Then a third shot, and closer still.

Suddenly there was some movement among the brush. It was a deer—and moving falteringly toward me. I raised my rifle and was about to fire when the deer appeared to simply fall over.

Then followed a thrashing in the brush along with some shouts (expletives deleted), and George's blaze orange form emerged into an opening. His rifle was not visible. Rather, he was brandishing his large buck knife as he ran toward the downed deer. Then, as he approached it, the buck staggered to its feet and took several jumps in my direction.

I moved quickly toward the action, and as I did, George launched himself upon the deer and took it down.

(More expletives by George, deleted.)

I was now upon the fury and saw the buck kick outward several times, one of his hind feet taking George squarely in the right cheek.

Then the buck shook him off, rose again and took several faltering steps to our right.

"George, where's your gun?" I shouted.

"Lost the d— thing in the snow back there," he yelled, looking a little dazed as he headed full-tilt for the deer once more.

"Stop!" I yelled. "I'll finish him off for you. You drew first blood and he's still your deer."

"No! This guy's mine," came the perhaps overly-determined reply. And he literally jumped on the deer again. And this time his knife found its mark, with the buck quivering out for the last time.

With the deer finally stilled, George looked up at me, his eyes sort of glazed and wild. "I got him," was all he said. Then he just sat there on the six-pointer with a silly grin on his face, which somehow made its way through the rivulet of blood that flowed down his cheek and along his mouth.

"Come on," I finally said. "Let's dress him out and drag him back to camp. We'd better get you patched up too, and we'd better locate your rifle."

Well, George started to get up and then sat back down as he began to inspect the several wounds in the deer.

"I was just wondering how I'm going to explain all this at the DNR check station," he then blurted out, looking up at me in bewilderment.

I thought a moment before replying, "You'll certainly have them confused when they find one bullet hole and five stab wounds in it... Then of course you could tell 'em you shot the deer with your buck knife, and by the time they figure out what sort of rifle a buck knife is, heck, we'll be back home!"

So off we went to locate George's rifle and put the deer on the buck pole…And oh yeah, just in case you're wondering, it did happen.

Bad Advice, Lousy Roads and
an Ex-Brother-in-Law

"You take M-196 off the Nirvanna Road for about five miles west 'till you come to an old dilapidated farm house," the duck hunter told me. "Then you turn back north and follow the old county line road 'till you see a two-track off to your left.

"That trail leads right to Lost Lake, an' it's where the ducks are flocking during the early part of the season."

I was at a Ducks Unlimited banquet when this took place, and had decided to try something a little different—besides wandering about with my camera and scarfing down prime rib.

So I edged about various tables asking the usual likely-looking suspects where to duck hunt.

Now, I've always had the idea that duck hunters were honest. Not any more. They're just like fishermen! You know, a guy brags about the fish he landed yesterday and you ask him where he caught 'em. Then his face suddenly takes on a sort of magical, ingenuous, poker-like expression as he explains how to get to some remote, dried-up swamp about seven counties away.

Well now, I left that first individual and confronted several more suspects before finding another likely-looking winner.

I shot him the same query.

The fellow turned and cocked his head sideways as he shifted his drink from one hand to the other, then gave me one of those stares like I was a squirrel after a nut.

Finally, he says, "Around here I really don't know for certain. I just moved to the area from Oregon a year back. But I can tell you of a guy that will know exactly where that Duck Lake you mentioned is at. You go north to M-287 and turn right 'till you come to the corner of Greenwing Road. There you'll see Bob's Place right on the corner. It's a small 'ol country store, but 'ol Bob's been around there for years, an' he'll steer ya straight to that Duck Lake.

"And say, that little lake is just loaded with ducks. I limited out there three days in a row last season—my first Michigan duck season, too."

I moved on, and although I'd ferreted out several other likely sounding locations during the evening, decided Duck Lake was for me.

So I began my search. And yes, there really is a Greenwing Road, but rather than stop and ask "'ol Bob" directions I set out on my own. But after following several old trails that led to some excellent deer hunting territory and a few swamps with not an ounce of hydrogen 2, oxygen 1, I turned back to Bob's Place.

Sauntering by the lone gas pump in my cammo outfit, acting for all the world like a real duck hunter, I wandered in and through a couple of rows of fishing tackle and old pots and pans. And there at the counter stood Bob himself—one of my sister's ex-husbands!

"Why, if it isn't Ed!" he exclaims, extending a grizzled hand. "Boy, you're really out of your territory up here, aren't you?"

"Good to see you too, Bob," I sez. And I suppose momentarily I was. "Didn't know you were up here in God's country. This your place?"

"Guilty as charged," he grinned back. "Wanna buy it?"

So we joked around a little before I told the old geezer the reason I'd stopped in was to find Duck Lake.

"No problem," he replied with a wry smile. "Duck Lake's only about a mile east of here."

"See," he pointed across the road. "That old dirt road over there takes you straight to it. Place should be bristling with feathers about now."

So I purchased a pack of stale peanuts, thanked Bob, and headed east. The result was that I wandered back and forth over that old dirt road for several hours, and no Duck Lake came to view.

Then with temper and dendrites frizzled, I stumbled across a real highway and headed back south.

"Heck," I sez to myself and the old truck, "I'm going back down home and shoot some ducks!" And that's just what I did, because the ducks were almost in my back yard.

But ah, the wonderment of it all—bad advice, lousy roads, ex-brother-in-law, and all for free. So from now on I'm just going to become one of the 'usual suspects' myself... Then again, should you really want to know where the ducks are, you go east to Fibber's farm. Then you turn south and pass the old oak stand 'till you come to an old pine stump, and....

Becoming a Politically Correct
Huntsperson and Fisherperson

S ince some of the state, federal and private sectors are managing to legislate away nearly every element for the living of a good and sensitive lifestyle through their demands for political correctness, I'm obliged, as an old-fashioned woodsperson, to take up my overtaxed processor of words and explain why my outdated mental resources have finally rendered me cerebrally marginalized.

You see, as the years have sped away, I've become more advanced in non-health, and eventually I know I'll be rendered non-viable. But while I am still able to ignore the negative impact of meat consumption on my health, and the social problems along with the new ecology of our society, I wish more than ever to feel like a hunter and fisherman rather than a huntsperson, a fisherperson, or even a woodsperson. Also, I feel it imperative that these words be properly processed while I may still be the owner of a non-human animal skin vest and cap.

I've always excelled at making fish and other game mobility non-possessors—in other words, killed them. Perhaps that's because I'm at times kindness-impaired, due to my upbringing and socialization. My natural birth mother passed on when I was three, and I was raised by my father-of-natural and my mother-of step. I had two brothers and three sisters-of-natural, along with two each sisters and brothers-of-step, and we all existed quite anthropomorphically in an age-depreciated farm house near the north woods.

So, as a boy I learned to tote a gun through the woods and to shoot game. Of course, then I was unhampered by rigid traditionalist ideals, while also being wisdom-challenged and logically under-enhanced.

In the fall and winter, my brothers and brothers-of-step and I all became wood-fuel technicians—that is to say that when we weren't hunting or fishing, we'd cut wood and haul it in for the cooking and for the pot-bellied deliverer-of-heat.

And many a time as a lad I wandered the streams with my rod-of-fly-fishing and a nongender-specific canine animal companion I called "Hey you!" This caused me to love to eat fish, but thermally enhanced venison steak was always my favorite dish. But it was always best when properly grilled—that is to say that I'd place it down before me and demand of it answers to a lot of ignorant questions. My mother-of-step always said that I was optically challenged and in need of glasses when I did that.

So over the years I learned to hunt non-human animals, and this made me become a huntsperson with rather expansionist ideas, as I rambled far and wide over the country-of-north. Yet I always tried to live in peace and self-determination. And in order to do that I've kept my ecological footprint downsized, while trying not to let others evade my caprinal space. It's a challenge to do that when one is both an economically disadvantaged and marginalized individual, and particularly so when one is also somewhat vertically challenged—only 5-foot-9—a standard of nonheight these days.

One of the most challenging problems was that as perhaps the least chronologically accomplished in my family, I at times became very odor-enhanced and dirt-accomplished while hunting or fishing. And I'm quite certain that my physical-intimidation prerogative passed away when confronted by my siblings. However, it didn't make me socially dysfunctional. Nope. I went right back into the stream or walked out through the leaf-of-color bushes to my favorite fishing or hunting spot.

So I've grown step by step into a culturally tolerant, morally righteous, intellectually astute and politically correct sexist male. But although I sometimes have testosterone-heavy thoughts, I don't feel morally out of the mainstream. I am, however, somewhat decorum-impaired. I muddle my way through though, like most of us, to what I trust will be my manifest destiny.

So over the years I've honestly tried to become an enlightened person with a healthy lifestyle, although it has been mentally anguishing to rely on a mostly fat-free, sodium-free diet of nuts and berries.

The upshot of all this is that I'm going to remain a huntsperson and a fisherperson, and I'll try my best not to be an imperialistic oppressor or willfully invade anyone else's personal life—so in light of that I'll end this writing soon,.

But why then, you may wonder, do I warp your eyes and brain by writing in such a sesquipedalian manner of enhanced strangeness? Well, I assure you that I'm not under the alkafluence of inkahol as I write, but rather it's akin to seeing a bow-legged cowboy and having to ask, "What manner of men be these, who wear their legs in parentheses?"

Writer's Note: I'm certain I read some of these politically-correct terms somewhere over the years, but some are my own interpretation.

Our Immune System Needs Humor

Some folks prefer to read informative stuff about hunting and fishing in any writing. Others enjoy stories of the out-of-doors that include some adventure, narrow escapes or a touch of the melodrama and suspense.

I try to do all of the above. However, still others say they enjoy a mix of humor too. And those folks may join me anytime on one of my hunting or fishing forays. The reason is simple, as I've always reckoned that one occasionally needs a downpour of humor along with a few drips of reason. Even if the humor is a little slapstick.

And findings seem to bear out the idea that cranking up your humor, perhaps as you're even cranking up a nice fish, also cranks up your immune system.

Now, haven't we always known or at least suspected this? And most writers have always known it, for good reason. When one writes for the public at large they become critically aware of two things. First, it doesn't take a rocket scientist to figure out that an outdoor columnist in general writes for the hunter or fisherman, but that he or she had better gear it up for the general public as well. And secondly, a little humor—maybe a lot on occasion—or even an adventure here and there, spices things up a little and makes it more palatable for all.

Ah, but there is one discovery a writer makes, and that is that one can't please every critic… Which reminds me of the Irish setter that sauntered into an ice cream parlor, laid down fifty cents and demanded, "Gimmee a double dip of chocolate!"

"That'll be two bucks," said the soda jerk.

"Sorry," said the dog as he tossed more money on the counter. Then he took his ice cream and started to leave.

"Wait," remarked the perplexed waiter, "we don't get many talking dogs in here."

"Well now, that doesn't surprise me a pheasant feather," the dog replied as he exited. "And at two bucks for an ice cream cone you aren't likely to see any more in here, either!"

Oh yeah, it seems that nearly everybody is a critic, or at least misunderstands your intentions... Like the time I'd figured out my taxes and asked my wife to please type at the bottom of the form, "the preceding taxes were figured with a slide rule." (Of course, that was back when everyone knew what a slide rule was.) Well, I glanced at the form just prior to mailing it and found that she'd typed, "The preceding taxes have been figured with a sly drool." Well, maybe they were at that, but I still felt like the angry inch worm who'd just been told to convert to the metric system.

I didn't chastise my wife though. After all, I need those instant TV dinners in order to survive. In fact, I've had so many of them I've developed a conditioned reflex. I see a piece of plastic and right away I get hungry.

But I must tell you that humor can lead you off in some strange directions. For example, one night after giving a speech laced with humor, I was asked to accept an important job down in Lansing. But I turned it down, figuring that too many folks were already flocking down there to ask what they could do for our state—and what the salary would be.

And yes, humor can also bring a family, or even a group of hunters, closer together. About the only thing that brings them closer together is a small pickup truck and three dogs. But the dogs are usually quite noble about it and ride in back. Speaking of noble dogs, I guess the noblest of all dogs is the hot dog—it feeds the hand that bites it, does it not?

So do you feel better now? I hope so, as I've told you a few stinkers and am optimistic that your immune system is cranked up a bit... Well, I'm optimistic.

'To the End of the Line, Laddie!'

While I'm not really at the end of my line, neither am I really in the mood to write about fishing today. Actually, I'm in one of my clean-up or desk-cleansing moods. So please cut me some slack in my fit of foolishness as I cleanse some stuff from the piles of papers on my desk.

Well now, speaking of cleansing an area, a fishing friend, Walt, dropped in the other evening. He glanced at a copy of a poem I wrote long ago and scoffed, "You're an outdoor writer. You know, huntin' and fishin' and all that. Ain't writing a poem a little sissyish?"

I didn't answer right away. Instead I relocated what remained of a six-pack on my desk further away from his clutching fingers as I tried to think of a stinging comeback.

I finally thought one up. "Strange or sissyish," I said. "I hear that you make rattattoie with real rats. Now that's what I'd call strange stuff!"

Now then, Walt tried to hide a look of disgust, then he grabbed up my six-pack of Coke and ran out of my office. Haven't seen hide nor hair of 'em for more than a week!

If you're at all interested, the poem he referred to is called "The Cleansers" and goes like this:

They've cleansed the area of all smoke, they've cleansed the drunks of drink. They've cleansed all prayer from schools—a joke! Next they'll be cleansing me, I think.

I guess ol' Walt didn't appreciate the bit of wit, but The Friendly Flier published it. Ah, but who cares? A writer simply writes, and most of them about a lot of different things. Perhaps I could repeat what Robert Benchley once said: "It has taken me 40 years to discover that I have no writing talent, but fame now will not let me give it up."

Then again, who knows what people are really like? And there's an old saying about that, which goes something like this: If you study books you will know how things ought to be, but if you study people you'll know how things really are… And things are really dry since Walt waltzed off with my Coca Cola.

Returning to the real world, what was it I started to write about today? Oh yes, about cleaning up the scraps of paper that clutter my desk. And such may make my afternoon useless. Ah, but how does that other old saying go? Yep, "If you can spend a perfectly useless afternoon in a perfectly useless manner, you've really learned how to live." Man, am I living today!

Please continue to bear with me, as I've seen some rather rotten writen' in my time. But this writen' may be written so rotten it can hardly be read! And, although it isn't intended as such, I may as well continue along this self-destructive path.

Ah, here's a scrap of paper that contains an item which may help to save this column—or perhaps kill it. And after transposing it, I'll put it in the deep six!

I call it "The End of The Line."

A Scottish hunter walked out of the woods and onto a village street, where a large funeral procession was passing by. First came a horse-drawn hearse, and a man and his faithful dog walked behind it. Then, along came about 200 people, stretched out behind them.

The hunter was indeed curious, so he walked up and inquired of the last person in the line, "Say, and would ye be tellin' me who this funeral is for?"

The fellow replied, "I don't actually know the person. Ye'll have ta ask on up the line."

So the curious hunter ran halfway up the procession and tapped another guy on the shoulder. "Say, my good man, and would ye be tellin' me who this funeral is for?"

The man replied, "Ye'll have ta ask the man up there wi' the dog."

So the hunter finally caught up with the man and dog and inquired once more, "Beggin' yer pardon sir, but would ye be tellin' me just who this funeral is for?"

Well, tears rolled down the other fellow's checks as he turned to reply, "'Tis fer me poor mother-in-law. You see, me dog bit 'er, and she died the very next day."

The Scottish hunter thought for just a moment before asking, "Say now, and would ye be lettin' me rent your dog for a day?"

"Aye, laddie, I'd like ta help ye," the man with the dog replied, pointing a thumb over his shoulder, "but ye'll have to go to the end of the line."

And that, faithful readers, is the end of the line for today. I've got to finish cleaning up this desk. And after all, you can't expect me to write serious stuff all the time ... can ye now?

The San Francisco 'Peking Duck'

Ducks here. Ducks there. Ducks everywhere! That's what it was like in Foster City, one of the many suburbs along the Gold Coast I was visiting in the San Francisco area.

To set the scene, wife Gerri and I recently returned to Michigan from Frisco, where we visited our daughter Mary and our new grandson, Edward.

But we traveled about the area, and found that many species of birds and animals frequented it besides ducks. There was a wide variety of wildlife at the zoo of course, and around the Stanford University campus as well.

However, I'm certain that Ducks Unlimited members will be happy to know that ducks were not only on Half Moon Bay but in almost every moat and pond for miles around. They even frequented daughter Mary's yard.

Which leads me to the subject matter herein.

That is that the most renowned duck of those within the San Francisco area was the one the locals now call "the late, great Peking Duck."

The account goes that a neighborhood Chinese gentleman returned from China, and brought back a new wife who was quite unaccustomed to California rules or law.

Now then, one very large mallard frequented the area where they lived. It was quite a pet throughout their neighborhood, actually able to be hand fed by grownups and kids alike.

During the second week back in the United States, the Chinese Gentleman returned home from work to discover duck feathers all about his front yard, and even scattered throughout the middle of his house. The man had actually come home early because he was excited to see if his wife had properly prepared his favorite meal, Peking duck. She had promised to do that.

Well, the trail of duck feathers led to the kitchen. And there his wife stood, proudly holding out a dish that no man could ever refuse. She gave him a toothy grin and proclaimed, "Peking duck fo' eat!"

To wrap it up, it seems the neighborhood forgave the poor lady after some time, but the legend of the San Francisco Peking Duck still lives on.

On to the trip itself...We've flown to California and other places along the 'left' coast several times. But what can one really see from 40,000 feet in the air? Not much, so this time the little woman and I decided to travel by the Amtrak train, the California Zephyr.

It was indeed quite an experience. The scenery was fantastic, and you meet some very interesting folks along the way. For example, a guy from Ohio who runs a summer camp for kids, a man and wife team headed for Colorado to trout fish, a young man on his way to Oregon to help a brother he hadn't seen in years construct a fish pond, a lady from Sacramento who manages an H&R Block office but is on her way back from Phoenix where she visited a son, and on and on.

However, the most unforgettable character I met during the trip was a man named Luther Jones. It was during the return trip, and I spent a good share of time helping the 70-year-old find his way about the train and keeping track of his little blue traveling bag. You see, Jones was obviously suffering from some form of dementia, and most of the time had no idea where he was or what was going on.

But during one of our many conversations I learned that Luther had at one time spent 23 years in the U.S. Air Force as a cryptographer in Empire, Michigan.

Luther said he was traveling to Pittsburgh, his old home town, so I told him farewell in Chicago, hoping that someone else would assist him in finding his way home. Others surely would, or at least I hoped so, for Luther Jones was not only confused but was quite bedraggled and I suspect, homeless as well.

So the trip to San Francisco and back was quite an experience, and of all those things we experienced two items really stand out...Luther Jones is one, and the other is the late, great Peking Duck!

Flagon with the Dragon,
or Vessel with the Pestle?

That great actor Danny Kaye once tried to memorize the following during one of his old movies: "The potion with the poison's in the flagon with the dragon, while the vessel with the pestle has the brew that is true."

A bit confusing, yes?

But wait a moment. If you relate that drivel to the countrywide fight for hunting and fishing rights and the multitude of wildlife so-called 'protection groups,' you could come up with something like:

"Preserving may be promising to the sources with resources, while the hunters and the fishers are the differential wishers."

So, if you substitute the various environmental groups and protection agencies as the 'sources with resources' and you and me as the 'differential wishers', tell me if you can, which has 'the brew that is true?'

Bet you can't. And neither can I. But I can see what is happening on the overall stage. That is, if we're not protecting our rights, we hunters and fishers are going to become the eventual losers. Fact.

The quandary comes when we realize that with population pressure, some lands, waters and wildlife need to be protected or refuged. And many of us have long advocated that without such, and nationwide, expansion and land-grabbing will eventually leave little space in which to pursue our out-of-doors activities.

Well, I've not been astonished upon noticing that state and national groups have continued to place more land and waters under their 'protective' wings. However, there are presently more than 500 wildlife refuges across this nation, and the list continues to grow. While parallel to this, the number of organized private wildlife protection and propagation organizations have continued to multiply, mostly in an effort to provide game and fish for the future—Pheasant Forever, Ducks Unlimited, etc.—the list seems endless, and I believe in what most of them stand for and do.

But somewhere and sometime, these two types of organizations are destined to clash. Fact is, they do so now. For, to a degree, although some may be unaware of such, they are diametrically opposed to one another.

My reasoning? Well, wildlife refuges are just that, and nearly all either drastically limit or completely deny fishing and hunting. Sporting clubs or groups, on the other hand, are comprised almost exclusively of men and women who are fishers or hunters. So, as the old saying goes, "somewhere, somehow, something's gotta give." Because after all, there's only so much water and land.

Meanwhile, federal and state management units and various local bureaus such as the U.S. Fish and Wildlife Service, state conservation departments, etc., all seem to be heading, perhaps unintentionally, in the same direction—that of total control over hunting and fishing and land and water use.

In my wildest dreams, as an outdoorsman, I cannot imagine a sharper two-edged sword. We 'differential wishers' run about performing various duties to protect and propagate wildlife, only to one day have the right to hunt or fish removed by the 'sources with resources'???

Well, the bottom line seems to be that the various wildlife protection agencies, national and state, have really been in control all along. Some say they should have been, and should remain so. However...

Where does that leave you and me? The answer is the reason for writing this, perhaps somewhat unpopular, item.

We must remain alert to any and every new land law or ruling that is about to be passed or is under consideration by the 'sources with resources'—those rulings that could affect our out-of-doors activities. And we need to continue our own organized activities, not only for the benefit of wildlife but to be present and have our say when the need arises.

Real world is, if we do not stay on the alert, we may one day find ourselves drinking from the 'flagon with the dragon!'

A Dark and Stormy Weekend

New Year's Day was getting closer, but I wanted to get involved in a little more of the archery deer season. However, I was in for a good shock as I peered out a window.

A blizzard was going on out there.

Actually, I was reminded of the 19th century English novelist George Bulwer-Lytton, whose book, Paul Clifford, begins with the much abused sentence, "It was a dark and stormy night." Or was it Snoopy the dog in that comic strip I thought of?

What I was certain of was that my two brothers, Ross and Don, along with myself, have weathered some pretty wicked weather during a few of our winter trips to the cabin. Well, maybe not this weekend in this storm.

You know, it seems we do some rather crazy things during our youth that are negated as we mature. Why? Well, I guess one advantage age has over youth is that youth knows little about getting old, whereas the old know all about being young.

Yes, we're only young once. After that we need to think up a new excuse.

I recall vividly one of our trips north to the cabin during the winter. We were quite prepared, or so we thought. We even hauled along a snowmobile just in case, and there wasn't a bit of snow until we got within a few miles of the cabin. At that moment we ran into what was a real whiteout, with about two-foot snowdrifts in the back roads.

There was no way we could drive the truck down the remaining half-mile trail to the cabin. But aha, the snowmobile. We unloaded the machine off the trailer and it immediately sank clear through to the ground and wouldn't budge.

Brother Ross, who always has a remark or answer for almost any situation, grinned and said, "Yes, life expectancy is most certainly increasing. Nowadays you can expect anything to happen."

Brother Don countered, "Well, you can simply smile. But if you smile when everything goes wrong you're either a nitwit or a repairman. So which are you?"

"Hey you characters," I said with sort of a scowl, "We've been all through this before. But remember, amnesia patients must pay in advance. So I guess here's where we pay."

And, shouldering most of our gear, we did pay as we plodded and stumbled our way through the blizzard to the cabin.

The first order of the evening was to get a fire going in the old wood stove. That accomplished, we kept keen eyes out through a window toward the swamp. We knew they'd hear us come in and would be there soon.

"They" would be deer, squirrels, raccoons and birds that invariably showed up looking for a handout whenever we came to the cabin. This entire event took place two years before the current baiting ban, so we were able to shovel a small area and spread out some corn and carrots.

And even with the bad weather, in they all came to enjoy a meal. We watched with interest as they came, some to stay for a little while and others for up to an hour or so. We knew that due to the weather there'd be little if any hunting this weekend. But watching wildlife itself is almost as much fun.

The weather took a a turn for the better and by that Sunday we were able to drive the truck in and head for home. But for the better part of two days we had simply relaxed, hiked short distances, told numerous stories and jokes we'd mostly heard before, and ate steaks and other great food in the manner in which kings must have plagiarized in their day.

Never mind that no actual hunting or other out-of-doors activities had taken place. We'd experienced one of the most quiet and enjoyable winter weekends ever at the cabin.

So perhaps being snowed in, or out as it may have been, can have certain advantages at that. However, as I glance out of the window into the "dark and stormy night" once again, I realize there will be no trip this weekend.

'Game' Keeps Getting in My Way

I suppose you'd say it's a no-brainer for one to concentrate on hunting and fishing this time of year, as hunting is still in vogue and some cold weather fishing isn't that bad, either.

Well now, I have a problem with either sport each year at this time. A real quandary it is, as something else seems to wreak havoc on my outdoor lifestyle.

Guess what! It's that game of football—Monday night football, Thursday night football, Friday night football, and even Saturday and Sunday football. That crazy game puts a wild bent in my schedule each year at this time.

Now, for those who don't know or didn't ask (and of course nobody doesn't or didn't), I've always been a football nut. I played four years of football in high school, called play-by-play radio for a college, announced home games for six years, coached the game seven years, and even reported it six years as a stringer for several media groups... Well, what a wonderful thing, eh?

So, in general, one could surmise that over the years I've made a nuisance of myself over that crazy sport.

But no longer. Starting right now, fishing, hunting and shooting sports will be my game. I'm even concentrating on those at the moment, as I happen to be scouting through the woods while looking for deer sign. And I'll even prove such as I write some resolutions in my playbook, er, notebook.

Resolve: I will no longer let football take over my outdoor life. Instead, I'll block it right on its back. I've simply got to pass it up and pursue other goals.

Resolve: From now on I will not be plugged in to a portable radio as I'm out here scouting players, er, deer. (Oh, oh! I'll have to take a time out right now, as I've just spotted a squad of deer. Ah, just as I thought, does 10, bucks 0). But what was that I just heard over my radio—Lions beat up again?

Resolve: I'll not drive my ORV over or through a DNR-created stump barrier or berm to get to my prime hunting area. I'll just surprise 'em with an end run instead.

Resolve: This season I'll not take advantage of any over-population of deer to take more than my limit. After all, it's not in a coach's, er, hunter's best interest to run up the score.

Resolve: I will practice Quality Deer Management (QDM) from now on. No shooting at the young ones; I'll simply pass those up for those with 10 points or better. That way, no one can accuse me of scheduling my games, er, shooting, to include those little teams, er, deer.

Oh, oh! I can now make out several deer through the brush ahead. Maybe I can sneak close enough to see if there are any real big ones in the huddle, or group, so I can key in on them later on.

Then again, maybe I'll just fake it to my tailback and go for a quarterback sneak. Could work, and you never know!

Enough, already! Time to get back to my Ranger and head for home, where of all things, we're having a block party. And I also understand that the Lions aren't about to show up, again.

Anyway, have a nice game, er day!

Black Bears Are on the Move

Throughout the northern United States the black bear population is growing rapidly, causing some outdoor minded folks to perhaps begin feeding on a 'bear' market... Except for the fact that there's no downward trend in their numbers. For example, it is estimated that at this time there could be upward of 15,000 in Michigan alone.

It seems that during the past 35 years the black bear has elevated its status from that of a pest to one of our most prized game species. And yet many people, even those who hunt the crafty animals, don't really understand bears.

It would require a book to cover everything, so I'm simply going to cover a few facts and hope they whet your appetite to learn more about our black bears.

Our black bear (Euarctos americanus americanus) resides in almost all of North America, from Nova Scotia and Labrador to west of the Rockies, and from the southern part of what we call the Northwest Territory south into Georgia, Alabama and Arkansas.

While you may spot a male bear almost anywhere, even in your back yard, it seems of late they range as far as 60 square miles, the females tend to range within a much smaller area of around 15 square miles.

The black bear's size, or of most any bear for that matter, depends upon its age, sex, diet and the season of the year. In most instances. An adult female (sow) is smaller than her counterpart. She will average

100-250 pounds, while the male (boar) can tip the scales anywhere from 150-400 pounds and occasionally more.

An adult black bear is an average of three feet in height when on all fours, and approximately five feet tall when standing. Perhaps I should clarify 'adult'. It means the bear's age when it's capable of reproducing, which averages two to three years of age.

While a black bear can live up to its mid-twenties, I have absolutely no idea where or how many of them pass on. As much time as I've whiled away in the woods of North America, I've never discovered a bear that looked as though it died of old age.

A black bear's diet is varied, as they eat most anything and everything. Vegetation is about 80 percent of its diet, while it also will consume nuts, berries, insects and even deer fawns and carrion. However, if available, it will plunder your pet food, garbage, or bird feed from your feeder. And an important item to remember is that it can also claw or slam through a building wall or window to get at stored items. With reference to that, feeding bears around a remote cabin or campground is not a wise idea.

Black bears normally breed in June or July, and cubs are born in January or February as the female winters. A litter may consist of one to as many as four cubs, two being the average. The sow normally breeds every other year.

At birth a cub may weigh as little as a pound, often less, but by spring they will be around ten pounds. They will tail their mother about throughout the summer months, and most will nurse until August. Then, near the end of fall the sow will again enter a den with the cubs, but the following spring she will aggressively discourage the (now) yearlings from following her. They are then off and on their own to learn the 'bear' facts for themselves.

And here seems to be where the 'pecking order' comes to play, as the older and larger male bears will have an established territory, and thus will sometimes aggressively chase off the younger bears. Now, perhaps that answers the question of why we see bears moving southward throughout the northern states. They are searching for their own territory perhaps? I believe so.

Can black bears be dangerous? Certainly, even though most are innately shy of humans and will run off when we appear in their area.

However, those that learn to associate food with humans are not apt to run far. Food overcomes their fear.

Yet, most times they run off. My son and I chanced upon one a few years ago while hiking along the Big Manistee River in Michigan. We actually smelled the bear before seeing it, as it had an odor like an old, musty rug. It was a big one, and arose about 50 feet in front of us before running off. We ran off in the opposite direction!

As another example, we were quite content with the fact that a big male black bear plundered our bird feeder at the cabin almost every evening. But one night I grabbed my camera and hid behind a woodpile that was about 15 feet from the bird feeder and waited. I wasn't disappointed. The huge male came in, reached up and shook the bird feeder, and then sat squarely down on his rump and began to shovel the seeds into his mouth. I then pointed the camera over the woodpile, took the snap, and watched but a moment as the bear rose up and looked squarely at me. I then retreated into the cabin at warp speed! The bear left quickly too.

Unless you're actually bear hunting, I'd recommend that moving away from a bear is the right choice—particularly should that bear be a female with cubs in the vicinity. She can become very protective.

One thing is for certain: bears are moving into new territory in consistent fashion, and we need to be aware of this and learn to deal with them when they suddenly appear in our stomping grounds. I guess that the old saying, "live and let live" is the better part of valor when it comes to black bears.

Do's and Don't's for Family Camping

There's still plenty of camping weather, and my family will probably do more of it. And I have many fond memories, and some not so great, of our camping excursions in Michigan's great outdoors.

No doubt about it, some of those visits to remote campgrounds have left a few indelible impressions on my mind, so I'd like to share a few "do" and "do nots" with you, so you and your family may experience a more enjoyable week or weekend by avoiding a few pitfalls that have at times all but swamped our little bundle of campers over the years.

So, in the words of the famed Jackie Gleason, "Away we go!"

First of all, remember that you can't trust a Michigan weather forecast, as it is the only place in the world you can go sledding and swimming on the same day. And it will undoubtedly rain, so be prepared for any weather and go at any time.

Attempt to secure a remote camp site if you are headed for any county, state or national campground. Don't pick out a location along a main drag, as Murphy's Law says that may land you in a straitjacket before your great experience ends.

See who's camping next to you as well. We traveled over 300 miles to get away from it all one time and wound up next door to some of our neighbors. Believe me, it was not old home week!

Do set up your trailer, camper or tent on the specific lot you've been assigned. Getting comfortable on the wrong lot may force you to enjoy a two-hour repositioning experience.

Do fill your fuel can with the proper gas if you're using Coleman or similar equipment for light and cooking. Should you ignore this warning and use fuel oil or gasoline, you will either have no warm experience whatsoever or you will experience the Big Bang Theory!

Do haul along some starter wood or kindling for fires. However, should you fail to do such, the kids can always cut some green wood from the forest. And that will cause a smoky experience, plus, the park rangers will be at your door.

Of course let the kids sleep outside in their sleeping bags... Wait, belay that transmission! It will most certainly rain during the night and the bedraggled and sopped little ones will sneak inside to take over your comfortable sleeping quarters.

Do prepare your fishing equipment in advance if near a lake or stream and are planning to rise early for some fishing. And do not let your waders, rod or other tackle sit outside during the night, for in the morning you may discover rusty reels, several inches of rain in your boots, or worse that a field mouse has chosen one of your boots for a nesting place.

Don't let fishing equipment lie about during the day. Extra fishing line, for example, left unguarded will not remain in one piece. It will surely be cut into small lengths and the kids will use it to pull their boats around in the water.

Do rise early and get in a quick shower and shave, but do not expect much of a campground restroom, if one even exists. The shower water will pop out in little icy beads and the electricity will normally be shut off. And you may also discover in the darkness that Solarcaine is not a substitute for toothpaste and that it is alarming to spray your underarms with a can of Off! bug spray!

Do store most everything inside at evening tide. If you let bait or food and drinks sit outside, in the morning you may find that raccoons have grabbed up your night crawlers and one-by-one dipped them in the half-gallon of milk you left open on the picnic table and devoured them all. Also you may discover that creatures of unknown origin have made off with the pop and other goodies you left outside in a cooler.

Do carry along some insect repellent and some sort of "sunshade." Don't splash on an after-shave or perfume, as insects of all shapes and sizes just love that stuff! Also, don't wear bright yellow clothing, as if there are bees in the area it will act like a magnet.

Don't leave garbage or food outside if you are in an area frequented by bears. If you do, you may fling open your door or tent flap to find yourself face-to-face with a black bruin or two. Now that could be an experience to write home about!

And finally, do take along a good first aid kit. Don't plan to use it, just be prepared.

There, now that I've filled your head with all these notions of impending gloom, I should add that probably none of the above will actually occur … So get out there in the rain and enjoy your camping experience!!

'Signs' of the Times

I heard of a Michigan farmer who once killed two birds with a single stone. He posted a sign that read: "Attention Hunters—Please Don't Shoot Anything on my Property That isn't Moving. It May be my Hired Man!"

I'll betcha the sign worked for hunters and the hired man.

But I recently saw another unusual sign—this one about taking out hunting insurance. Did you know you can do that? Take out hunting insurance on yourself? Before going deer hunting, for example, you can stop by an insurance company and insure yourself for a gadzillion dollars or so, whatever you feel you're worth. Well now, I know of a hunter who took out $500,000 worth of life insurance before going hunting. The upshot was that it didn't help him one bit—he died anyway!

The following really has little to do with signs, except that it may be called another "sign of the times." (You can see I'm having a little fun here, as I'm sometimes wont to do, please bear with me.)

It seems that deer had been reported as being shot within a certain area posted "NO HUNTING." So a conservation officer stopped a likely looking suspect that was speeding away from the area. First he told the driver he'd been speeding, then asked to see his driver's license.

The driver, who was indeed a hunter, replied, "Don't have a driver's license."

He was then asked for the automobile's registration and insurance papers.

"This is my wife's car," the hunter says, "and you'll find 'em in the glove compartment, along with one of my hand guns."

The CO was now not only astonished, but also was getting a little nervous. "What you got in the trunk?" he asked.

"There's two deer in there. I just shot 'em," the hunter implied.

Now the CO jumped on his radio, and soon there were two other officers on the scene. Following a discussion among the officers, one of them sauntered up to the hunter and said, "Now, listen carefully, I want to see your driver's license, this car's registration, and also need to see inside your glove compartment and trunk."

So the hunter pulled forth his driver's license and showed the officer the auto's registration and insurance. Then he showed him that there was no hand gun in the glove compartment, and quietly opened the trunk to reveal—nothing but a spare tire.

The CO was somewhat agitated and more than a little confused. "So tell me," he said to the hunter, "why did you tell this other officer that you had no driver's license, no registration, but had a hand gun in the glove compartment and two deer you'd shot in the trunk?"

The hunter replied with an innocent smile, "And I'll just bet the first officer told you I was speeding out of the area, too! Where do you get these guys, anyway?"

(Do you think it worked? Well, don't try it, 'cause it didn't!)

The usual modus operandi in today's decision-making, either to change the rules or put up signs, is to form a committee. And you may have heard that a camel is a horse designed by a committee. You didn't? Well, a committee will study, for example, the opening or closings of hunting or fishing seasons, limits, costs, along with the complexities, etc., etc. And it's my belief that such a committee should consist of no more than five people, four of whom remain eternally absent. Man, just think of the cost savings, the rapidity at which decisions could be made, and the simplicity of it all. Why, we might even be able to understand the decisions that come forth!

Gettin' lonely here! But did you know that scientists have proven that the older coal is, the better it becomes? Therefore, I guess you could say there is no fuel like an old fuel!

So, please forgive this old "fuel" for rambling on here. I guess the fact is that a column should be like a lady's dress—long enough to cover the subject but short enough to be of interest...Let's see now, what was that subject again?

The Eve of Deer Season

'Twas the eve of deer season, and all through the tent;
Not a person was stirring, 'seemed near heaven sent;
Each rifle was racked near the wood stove with care,
In hopes that the sunrise soon would be there.
The hunters were laying all snug in their beds,
While the snoring was raising the roof o'er their heads.
And I in my red longjohns and old hunting cap,
In spite of the noise was trying to nap,
When out mid the trees there arose such a crash,
That I sprang from my bunk and made a mad dash
To the doorway proclaiming, "Some silly old sinner!"
And what I saw then nearly cost me my dinner.
For what to my wonderment there did I see,
But an old Ranger truck piled into a tree.
'Twas rusty and beat up, but did it appear
That it's bed was all loaded with Icy-Cold beer?
Then the driver sprang out, and I thought I was dreaming,
For there stood a 12-point, with antlers gleaming!
He swaggered and laughed, a right jolly old stag.
And I asked right out loud, "Am I half in the bag?"
"Oh no," he replied, with a touch of a frown,
"I've one chore to do, then we'll all party down.
We must go inside and get straight to my plan,
And don't wake the others, they'll not understand."

Dumbfounded I watched as he went to his task,
Removing each trigger from the rifles, then asked,
"You won't tell them, will you? The idea you see,
Is to party all night as they can't come for me
Until they feel able, but then when they do,
They'll find they are missing a trigger or two."
I agreed with him then, and said it was fine,
As he'd left one untouched—and that rifle was mine!
Well, we woke all the others, and startled they were,
To find a great stag in their midst with no fear.
And "Here's a wonderful buck," they did cheer,
"For hasn't he brung us this party of beer?"
So we laughed 'round the campfire till morning was nigh,
And no one went hunting—some thought they may die!
Each hunter went stumbling instead back to bed,
Finally leaving just me and the buck, and he said,
"Well, I guess they'll stay out of the woods for today,
And that will grant time for my quick getaway.
But for your assistance, you may have my old Ranger,
I'll need it no more, for I'm now out of danger."
Then he turned and proclaimed as he sprang out of sight,
"Happy hunting to all, and to all a good night!"
Well, it must have been noon when I woke—what a dream!
For such just couldn't happen, or so it would seem.
I ran to the gun rack, and it just didn't figure,
That there on my rifle was the only trigger!
So then I snuck out of the tent like a cat,
And there 'gainst a tree the old Ranger sat.
I approached it with caution—in wonder 'twould seem,
And thought I was having another bad dream.
For there in the bed of the truck sat a can of Icy-Cold beer,
And laid out in a fan
Seven triggers off rifles—and I yelled with glee,
"What a deer season opener this is going to be!"

The Awesome Ride of Ross Revere

Listen all hunters and you shall hear
Of the awesome ride of Ross Revere.
'Twas 12 October, in sixty-five
And scarce a hunter is now alive,
To recall that scary night and year.

Just as the moon took flight from view
And the forest leaves fell quiet too,
A ghostly silence fell over the land,
But 'twas not for long, fate took a hand
As the scene was changed to one of fear.

Ross Revere sat high in an old oak tree
With longbow in hand and creaking knee.
He'd seen not a thing, time to get down
And join his partners over in town,
To tell tall tales about hunting deer.

Lowering his bow, he heaved a sigh,
While glancing toward the darkened sky.
Then, below was a motion, a little at first;
And Ross Revere now feared the worst
For it must be a bear, large for a deer!

To hug the tree, or creep on down?
A quandary thought he, casting a frown.
For if it were a bear, ah, therein lay the rub;
And more so perchance if it had a cub.
Still, he must see his buddies, back in town.

So Ross Revere stood quiet a while,
Then his face took on a gruesome smile
As he reached to his belt to pull a knife;
This blade, thought he, may save my life.
There's naught to fear, this is no strife!

But smile turned to groan as a knee gave out
And he fell from his stand with an awful shout.
He thought all was over but 'twas his luck,
He came squarely down on a 12-point buck
That snorted, woofed, and pranced about!

But only an instant did the buck so clown,
And then it put the pedal down,
While Revere hung on for breath and life
And thought in vain of his missing knife,
As the deer bee-lined it straight for town.

'Twas the wildest of rides or'e many miles,
Or'e logs and stumps, fences and stiles
And it was ten, by the village clock
That hung below the weathercock,
When hooves rang on the village tiles.

Folks sprang forth, looked on in fright,
As the fate of Revere rode in that night,
Toward the old church, down at the square,
Where the buck hit brakes, and Ross the air
To land in a heap, as the buck took flight.

Townfolk and partners ran to his side
To declare it was an awesome ride.
Revere then rose, and shed but one tear;
Not for himself but that now-famous deer,
He'd rode the distance that eventide.

But to this day, and to the last,
They'll discuss that evening of the past,
About a perilous time, and one of fear;
Of the hoof beats of that monstrous deer,
And the awesome ride of Ross Revere.

Curly Bear's Halloween 'Farce'

T he sun was setting in the western sky, and many of the forest animals were preparing for an evening of excitement.

It was the eve of Halloween, the night when all the ghosts and goblins were said to come out of hiding and roam about the forests. Except that tonight those eerie creatures would be young squirrels, raccoons and other animals, each dressed up in costume. They would knock on doors of other animals and would be trick-or-treating.

However, in the bear's den, Curly, the youngest of two siblings, was afraid and hesitant.

"Dad," he finally asked, "How are we going to know just who the ghosts and goblins are? Some of us will be dressed like them, and well …"

"Curly," father Harry Bear said as he continued to help Curly into a Darth Vader outfit. "You needn't worry. You'll be able to tell friend from foe. For example, Sammy Squirrel wouldn't be able to hide that big bushy tail under a costume. And how about Robby Raccoon. He's already wearing a mask and won't need a costume at all."

Young Curly Bear laughed at his father's remarks, but still he wasn't really satisfied. But ah, an idea suddenly flashed to his mind!

"I know," Curly growled, "I'll just zap any bad ones with my light-saber!" And he held up the long, heavy flashlight his father had given him to carry. He brandished it about, flashing its beam on and off.

Now Honey Bear, Harry's wife, was just finishing dressing up Fuzzy Bear in an owl costume. And we all know how mean owls can be. Why, they can scare off any ghost, and especially one the size of Fuzzy himself.

So Fuzzy took on a ferocious look for a moment as he tried to play the part. Then, he suddenly stopped short and stammered, "Whoooo,... m...m...me?"

Father bear laughed a second or two, then he became more serious and a little irritated. "Now look here, you characters," he admonished. "There will be nothing out there to be afraid of. Besides, I'll be walking a little behind you...Let's be off now. It's nearly dark."

Ah, but meanwhile in the wolf's den, Wylie Wolf was making his own plans for the evening. He'd not dress up in a costume, but simply hide behind a tree and grab up any trick-or-treater that passed his way.

Wylie was drooling as he rubbed his empty tummy. "What fine meals I'll be cooking up tomorrow!" And he stealthily left his den and crept deep into the forest. There he located a large, hollow stump, and enclosed part of its top and an entrance way with large, heavy sticks. Then he hid behind the stump, watching and waiting....He didn't have to wait long.

Soon, Wylie Wolf heard forest animals approaching and laughing as they knocked on doors to shout out trick or treat requests such as, "Trick or treat, smell our feet, give us something good to eat" and other laughable chants.

Well, the first to approach Wylie's stump were two mice, dressed as French cooks.

"Cooks?" growled the wolf. "I'll cook you two for my lunch tomorrow!" And he grabbed up the mice and stuffed them into the top of his prison stump. Then along came other animals—two squirrels, three rabbits and a possum. And he rapidly grabbed up all those and deposited them in his prison.

And now, along came Fuzzy Bear, dressed in his owl suit. He was followed closely by his brother Curly. Father bear was trailing somewhat behind them. Now these bears were somewhat larger animals than the wolf had expected, but still, he figured they'd be no match for his strength. So he sprang from behind his stump and grabbed Fuzzy by a paw.

Then Fuzzy Bear yelled out, "Help! Help me!"

Young Curly Bear hesitated for only a moment; then he jumped forward with his large 'light-saber' flashlight, shining it directly in the wolf's eyes. Then he raised the flashlight high and brought it down hard, directly between the wolf's eyes!

There was a loud thud as the flashlight hit and went out. But the wolf was out as well, and now lay on the forest floor.

Suddenly the bears heard cries for help coming from within the wolf's stump, and father bear moved in quickly. He crashed aside the sticks at the entrance with one sweep of a large paw, and the animals that had been captive were now free of the wicked wolf.

All the animals then gathered around young Curly Bear, thanking him for saving them from the wolf. "You're our hero, Curly!" they cried out.

"You saved Halloween for all of us, Curly," said father bear, as they ambled back down the trail toward home. "You were a good Darth Vader tonight, you and your light-saber. You are indeed a real hero!"

Then Curly giggled as he replied, "Maybe this costume is a farce, Dad. But if it is, the 'farce' has really been with me tonight!"

Helping St. Whitetail on Christmas Eve

The following story is especially for youngsters—but you may read it too.

Each year I try to write something about what it may be like when Christmas arrives in the animals' forest world. This one is new, for kids from 2 to 92. So from me to you and yours, be good to one another and have a very merry Christmas.

*   *   *

It was late evening on the night before Christmas in the deep forest and all the woodland creatures had long since snuggled down in their nests, lairs and caves.

The youngsters were dreaming about the toys and candy canes they'd find under their Christmas tree and in their stockings on the morrow good things that would come from a visit by St. Whitetail, their Christmas Santa.

Outside the snow was falling, sparkling like tiny stars in the occasional rays of moonlight that slipped through the clouds. It was crisp and cold, and the snow was getting deeper on the ground while its weight was beginning to bend the fir and oak branches downward along the forest path.

Mr. and Mrs. Bear had also settled down in their cave. But recalling last Christmas when he'd actually spoken to St. Whitetail, Mr. Bear decided he'd enjoy talking to the big charger once again. So he'd set his alarm for 4 o'clock in the morning, thinking that would be about the time St. Whitetail would come by with his deer and his sleigh full of gifts.

Well now, Mr. Bear's alarm went off on schedule so he arose and ambled over to his Christmas tree.

"Nothing's here!" he exclaimed. "Something must be wrong. St. Whitetail should have been in this part of the forest by now."

So Mr. Bear slipped on his warm boots. Then, carefully opening the door to his cave, he stepped outside and began walking quietly down the forest path while peering into the distance.

After a short walk he came across Wylie Coyote, who was standing outside his den. "Have you seen St. Whitetail?" he asked.

"Not hide nor hair!" snapped Wylie. "I guess the old guy forgot us this year."

"Not a chance," Mr. Bear replied in a pleasant voice. "I'm going to go in search of him. You'd better come along. He may be in trouble and need our help."

"No way," sneered Wylie. "I'm going back to sleep. So the coyote went back inside his den and slammed the door shut.

Mr. Bear continued down the path and soon came across Harry the Hare.

"Have you seen St. Whitetail?" he asked.

"Na," the hare answered. "I guess I'll just have to tell my 26 kids and 208 grandchildren that he's not coming this year. Why? Are you looking for him?"

"Yes, I'm looking for him. Maybe he needs help," replied Mr. Bear, his voice showing some anger. "And maybe, just maybe, you should come along too. Tell you what, if you don't come along and help maybe I'll make sure you're 'hare' today and gone tomorrow. How would you like that?"

Now then, Mr. Bear was much larger and more powerful than Harry the Hare, so the rabbit reluctantly closed the door to his home and followed Mr. Bear down the path.

Soon they came across Stinky Skunk, who was also peering into the darkness.

"Stinky, have you seen St. Whitetail?" asked Mr. Bear. "We think he may be in trouble and in need of our help."

"I've not seen him," answered Stinky. "But a while ago I heard some strange noises down this path. Like calls for help or something like that, but I'm not going to go looking for trouble."

"Too bad," said Mr. Bear. "Harry the Hare and I are searching for St. Whitetail. We think he may be in trouble and in need of our help."

So bear and Hare continued down the forest path. On their way they were able to gather up a few other animals that would help. Soon Freddy Fox, Bernie Buck, Ricky Raccoon and Crafty Cougar became part of their rescue team.

Suddenly they saw it—a huge sleigh piled high with bags while tilting dangerously to one side. It was stuck in a large drift of snow and eight white-tailed deer were trying desperately to pull it free.

St. Whitetail himself was in the driver's seat, attempting to coax his deer onward. He was a large, lean and lanky deer, and atop his head sat very large, many-pronged antlers.

Mr. Bear charged in. "Come on," he ordered the other animals. "It is St. Whitetail and he needs our help."

So Mr. Bear pushed behind the sleigh while the others pulled up front with the deer. Soon the sleigh slid free of the snow bank.

Then St. Whitetail looked each of the helpers over very carefully and said, "I know each of you good folks and I also know where you live. Thank you for your help and you will all have a great Christmas day."

And it was so. All those who'd helped free his sleigh returned to their homes to find many fine presents under their Christmas trees and in their Christmas stockings.

But what about Wylie Coyote? He found one thing tied up in his stocking on the door of his cave—it was Stinky Skunk, fast asleep.

Mr. Bear thinks of Christmas.

Mr. Bear's Christmas Wish

Author's note: Whether or not we're hunters or fishers, I'm quite certain we all harbor respect for the fur and feathered creatures of this earth. Thus, I'm presenting this Christmas story for all outdoor-minded kids, from 2 to 10, with a "Very Merry Christmas to you and yours." It's something to read to your little ones.

It was Christmas Eve in the deep forest, and all was hushed and very still. The forest creatures were snuggled down in their nests, lairs and caves while outside a light snow was falling, sparkling like tiny stars in the patchy moonlight.

The animal and bird youngsters were all dreaming of the good things they'd find in their Christmas stockings upon the morrow, and those goodies would most certainly come from a visit by Saint Whitetail, their Christmas Santa.

Mr. and Mrs. Bear had settled down in their cave somewhat earlier. They'd prepared for a long, wintry nap.

But suddenly Mr. Bear was awakened and somewhat startled by a growing clatter of sounds out on the forest floor. Then he listened intently and heard other hushed yet joyous noises approaching outside his cave.

At first Mr. Bear thought the noise may be Ricky Raccoon and his family, out partying and rummaging about in the garbage cans. And this thought made him quite angry.

Rubbing the sleep from his eyes, Bear threw open the door to his cave and grumbled, "If that's Mr. Raccoon I'll give him the dickens for making such a racket—and on Christmas Eve, too!"

Then Mr. Bear saw in the distance, but fast approaching, a large sled being pulled by eight whitetail deer. Its drive was lean and lanky, and atop his head was a set of very large, many-pronged antlers.

"Why, it must be Saint Whitetail himself!" Mr. Bear uttered under his breath. "This is indeed an honor, for very few have ever seen him!"

Then Mr. Bear stood still and watched from his doorway, and can you guess what he saw?

Saint Whitetail stopped at each nest, nook and lair,
And at each he left brightly wrapped baskets to share.
He left nuts for the squirrel and meat for the owl,
Sunflowers for the rabbit and seeds for the fowl.
He left food for the lot of them—rich and the poor,
Then reigned in his chargers to stop at Bear's door.
He leaped from his sled, a right jolly old stag,
"And what would you like, Mr. Bear, from my bag?"

Well now, as one may imagine, this entire scene plus Saint Whitetail's question caught Mr. Bear somewhat in awe. Still, Mr. Bear was a kindly and thoughtful one, and he hung his head for a brief moment, almost as though in prayer. Then came his reply.

"Well, if wishes came true, and I had my wishes,
There'd be food for all deer and clean water for fishers;
There'd be cover for all of the pheasants and rabbits,
And no dumping of trash, or other bad habits.
There'd be food for the fall, the winter and spring
Why, Christmas each day would be just the thing!"
This made the stag smile, then his face grew quite wise,
And the glint of a tear seemed to form in his eyes;
Then he softly responded, and this he replied:
"Mr. Bear, for the animals, birds and all fishes,
Unknown to yourself you now have all your wishes.
There are many conservationist folk, you should see,
For the fish and the fowl and the ground and the tree.

Pheasants Forever, Whitetails, 'Unlimiteds' too.
  Why, they're already doing as you wish them to do.
And beyond that, you know there are habitat studies,
That work for the better for you and your buddies.
So worry about nothing, not even a man,
  Think 'Christmas' each day, live the best that you can."

Then Saint Whitetail paused and watched Mr. Bear's eyes grow brighter and brighter as the feeling of a Christmas wish fulfilled came over him. Then the big stag smiled as he said, "I won't be leaving any special Christmas gift for you this year, Mr. Bear. You already have one, and yours is a gift for all the forest animals and birds."

"Your gift-wish was wise, and you've answered a call,
  So you see, Mr. Bear, you've the best gift of all."
Then Saint Whitetail sprang to his sled, giving a nod,
And away they all flew, like the dandelion pod.
But Bear heard him exclaim, "Moms, dads, sons and daughters –
  Merry Christmas to all in the woods and the waters!"

The Day After Christmas

'Twas the day after Christmas,
and all through the house
    We picked up the pieces,
just me and my spouse.
    The bright colored wrappings
we'd done up with care,
    Were now all about, where
they'd flown through the air.
    The children still nestled,
all snug and a'sleep,
    Unaware of the mess they'd
created so deep;
    When out on the street
there arose such a roar,
    That I sprang to a window,
and then to the door.
    "The trash truck is here!" I
exclaimed in a shout,
    "So we've got to hurry and
get this stuff out!"
    We grabbed up and sacked
up, as fast as could be,
    Then ran to the truck, little
woman and me.

Ed Gilbert

The driver's eyes twinkled,
glancing over our trash,
    And then he just stood
there in total abash;
    Then finally he said, "Now
look here my good man,
    Here's a train set, a doll and
a little toy van;
    I don't wish to admonish,
but don't throw these away,
    Or the kids won't forgive you
'til next Christmas day."
    So he handed each back as
I took a good look.
    And the clothes that he wore
were all covered with soot;
    They had been bright red,
and trimmed in white lace,
    And his beard was all
tangled about his round face.
    He was chubby and plump,
and quite jolly was he,
    As he picked out the toys
and gave them to me;
    Then he faced his little helpers,
and called each by name,
    "Now Roger! Now Donald!
We'll find more of the same;
    More youngsters may have
the same problem, I fear,
    And we can't have them
wait for their toys all year."
    So off they proceeded, on
to the next house,
    And I glanced with
amazement at my little spouse;
    "Was that who I think it

was?" I asked unto her,
     "Just couldn't be," she said,
"But alas, I'm not sure.
     So we walked to our house,
and then stopped in the snow;
     For there on a step with a
bright-colored bow,
     Lay a large package, and
our names were there too;
     And a card read, "Merry
Christmas, from me unto you!"
     So we opened the package, and
what was therein?
     A photo of Santa,
wearing a grin.
     Then we heard a voice from
a distance, far away,
     "A Happy New Year too,
and all have a great day!"

Wiggles Wabbit—An Easter Fairy Tale

This tale is about a young rabbit, of course. But for our story let's just call him a 'Wabbit'. And, sometimes rabbits are called 'hares'. But again, for our tale, his name is really Wiggles Wabbit.

Little Wiggles was in grade school, and he was a good student—although he quite often forgot to mind his Mom and Dad. And one thing his Mom and Dad kept telling him, was always to take the sidewalk to school. "Never," they warned, "never take the short path to school through the forest. There are some very angry squirrels in those woods, and we don't want our Wiggles to get hurt."

But one morning Wiggles realized that he had to hurry or he would be late for school. He looked down the long sidewalk and then toward the shorter path through the woods. And, you guessed it, he went hip-hopping down the forest path.

Suddenly, much angry chatter came from the overhead trees, and Wiggles looked up just in time. For the squirrels began to throw things down at him. Down flew oranges and grapefruit and tomatoes, and other fruits. Well, Wiggles got so mad that he began to jump about to escape, and when he did he suddenly saw a squirrel on the ground in front of him.

With his large feet, Wiggles then began to jump and thump-thump-thump on the poor, little squirrel.

And, just then, down from a tall pine tree floated the good fairy!

"Wiggles Wabbit," she warned, shaking her magic wand in his face, "you are being a naughty little Wabbit. Your Mom and Dad have told you never to take this path through the forest, but to always take the sidewalk to school… And, you could have hurt this poor little squirrel."

"But," Wiggles squirmed in astonishment, "I was going to be late for school, and—."

"I know," the good fairy said kindly, "but you must remember never to come this way again, and to always mind your Mom and Dad."

"I won't do it again," said Wiggles, bowing his head.

"Then go back home and take the sidewalk to school," said the good fairy. "But just remember, if you do this again you will be a very bad little Wabbit."

So Wiggles returned to his home and jumped down the sidewalk to school. And Wiggles was a very good Wabbit for a few days. But then one day he saw that he was once again going to be late for school, and down the forest path short-cut he jumped.

And suddenly, bananas and watermelons and other fruits filled the air as the squirrels attacked. And, once again, Wiggles saw a little squirrel near him and began to thump-thump-thump on it with his big feet.

And again, down from the tall pine tree floated the fairy!

This time she was very upset with Wiggles Wabbit. She shook her magic wand in anger and said, "You have been a very naughty boy again, haven't you? You have taken the forest path and once again tried to hurt a little squirrel. You are behaving like a little goon, aren't you? Now, you go back to school the way you should… This is your second warning, and if you come this way again, something bad is going to happen to you."

"Yes, ma'am," squirmed Wiggles, and he jumped back home and down the sidewalk to school.

Well, Wiggles was a very good Wabbit for a few days. But then, one Monday morning he realized he was going to be late for school again. And you know what he did, don't you? That's right, he went jumping down the forest path!

Suddenly, grapes and peaches and pears filled the air as the squirrels attacked once more. And, once again, Wiggles saw a little squirrel nearby and began to thump-thump-thump on him with his big feet.

And then, down from the tall pine tree floated the good fairy!

"Wiggles Wabbit," she admonished, "you are not behaving as a little Wabbit should. Indeed, you do act more like a goon than a little hare. So I know just what I'll do."

The good fairy then waved her magic wand, and KAZAAM! Wiggles Wabbit was turned into a goon!

And so, my little friends, the moral of my little story is that you must always mind your Mom and Dad—for, if you do not, you could be 'hare' today and 'goon' tomorrow!

A Note to My Grandsons

B oys, I celebrated a recent birthday by repairing my old tree stand and helping a few other hunters do the same to their stands.

I'm now sitting on my stand as I make these notes. It is high in the branches of this old pine tree, and swaying in the early morning breeze. Dawn is just peeping over the horizon through the pine needles and rays of sunshine are filtering through onto my notebook.

I'm not up here to hunt today. Rather, I'm doing some scouting. But I did bring my bow along, just in case! However, it is simply a beautiful morning to be in the out-of-doors, and the possibility of seeing deer or other wildlife is charging my batteries and building up my enthusiasm.

And a deep part of my enthusiasm is for you boys to one day enjoy what I will enjoy on this moment in history.

The three of you are very young now. However, one day you will be 12, then 15, and onward. Just now you won't be reading this nor be able to understand anything herein, but I write to you now with the hope that, God willing, you will one day read this note and understand it.

In 50-plus years you will be the age I am now, and your world will be much different. So will the good-news/bad-news situation concerning hunting, fishing and other outdoor activities. The same may be true throughout the world.

No doubt that by the time you are able to understand these words, the environment will have already been an important part of your early education. You may even have a jump-start on it as well as a basic understanding of the conservation of our natural resources. A part of this curriculum may not only stem from your classroom but from each of your fathers, with whom I've hunted and fished many times over the years. Fact is, your fathers may by now have taken you on several hunting or fishing trips, perhaps not only here in Michigan but to some far-flung places throughout the united States that they and I enjoyed from time to time.

Perhaps you've enjoyed some fishing trips with your mom as well—each of them have out-fished me on many an occasion. And two of those fine ladies are also great hunters, so don't sell 'em short when it comes to handling firearms.

Boys, who knows what will happen within your lifetime? Surely I can't predict such, but I do know some of the things that have taken place in my lifetime. I'll give you a few examples.

My father first led me into the woods to hunt when I was a lad of twelve. We hunted snowshoe rabbits in a northwoods swamp, and it wasn't just the hunt, but the personal comradeship with dad that really mattered. I downed my first buck when I was the same age. And again, although the joy of success and the rush of adrenalin from a successful deer hunt was overpowering, I recall that the real joy stemmed from just being in the out-of-doors and the companionship and fun of being around those within our hunting party.

Ah, but things seemed so much simpler in those early days. There was the outdoor life to thrill us rather than television or video games, or the myriad of other novelties that clutter up lives today. And many items were either free or less costly than they are today or will be in your day. For example, land and water was more plentiful and open then for hunting and fishing. They'll be less so in your time. Perhaps, by the time you approach my age, you may only be able to hunt or fish as a private club member or only with permission to do so in private or leased areas. And I detest the idea, but perhaps you may not be able to hunt or fish at all. For there are now animal rights folks afoot that are distributing anti-hunting/fishing propaganda to school children all across the country. You most certainly will be able to read some of it by the time you're able to read this. I only hope such does not convince you to follow and support such beliefs.

For more than a hundred years, hunters, fishers, and sportsmen's groups have poured financial resources and sweat into the sound management and maintenance of wildlife in Michigan and all across the United States. They have done so, and continue to do so, in order to support the American tradition of an out-of-doors lifestyle. Please never let people who've never experienced our tradition to take it away from you. Someday that choice will be up to you.

Well boys, I must wrap this up. But it is a beautiful view from my old stand in this pine tree. The sun is now up, the squirrels are chattering around me, a coyote is yipping in the distance, and several deer seem to be working their way toward me. It is great, and I believe that someday you will be here with me—I wish this were the moment....
Grandpa Ed

Be Blessed By Our Great Outdoors

Someone once said, "Blessed is he that expects nothing, for he shall never be disappointed."

And you know, after writing several thousand columns and stories for various publications, it has dawned on me (like the youngster who waited up all night for the sunrise and it finally dawned on him) that I may never really be disappointed.

I've also heard it said that there is really nothing new to say or write about in this world, that it has all been said or written before.

But I believe that's wrong, and that is also the reason I've never really been disappointed with life. It all has to do with having an out-of-doors lifestyle.

You see, I've never met a real outdoors man or woman that I didn't like to be around. True, they may be one of those who can talk my arm off, but that doesn't bother me one iota. And that's because they always have interesting experiences and subsequent stories to relate.

Well, as some of you may have noted by now, I actually prefer story telling to straight reporting. And I can do some of each because being a columnist allows the opportunity of doing both.

So I feel somewhat blessed, and should you too like to be blessed by outdoor life I have a few suggestions.

First, when you're out among other fishers, hunters, shooters, etc., you are really among comrades. So listen to others and even encourage them to relate their experiences.

I don't care if they're telling a sad story, like the turtle who fell in love with the German war helmet for example, listen anyway. A story is history itself, and what really is history but perhaps a rearview mirror on the road of life. (I like that one, but do admit it isn't original).

Also, my advice is to never pass up a likely looking yard sale, garage sale or a flea market where old fishing tackle, hunting equipment or other outdoor gems may be lurking in wait. There is a story in each of those many castoff items, and if you listen carefully you can almost hear them talk, even though your wife or companion may be trying to get you to purchase a two-wheeled tricycle for the kids or grandkids.

For example, some years ago I began to collect old split bamboo fly rods, mostly from garage sales. Now I not only have several of them, but actually prefer to fly fish with them over my Orvis. Ah, but that's another story.

One more suggestion. Should you really want to become involved in our outdoor world, join one of your many outdoor organizations, whether a hunting or a fishing or a shooting group. If you do, you'll not only hear about the past present or future of outdoor life, you'll immediately become a part of it.

I want to follow this up with a question: Do you actually recall what you were worrying about a year ago today? No? Well, I don't recall that either, and for that matter, I don't really care. For I've found that worries simply disappear when I'm flipping a fly on some river or lake, or out on a cold winter fox-hunt, hiking the woods for small game, staked out for a gobbler to come strutting along, or even sitting over a runway chomping a Mars bar and waiting for that deer with antlers like a liar to come by.

Actually, I can then return to camp and listen as those other pals tell their tales of success, woe, or outright lies!

Well now, I'm aware that one important ingredient in a recipe for writing or story telling is "shortening." So I'll end this soon. However, please join with us folks who are involved in out-of-doors activities...You too may never really become disappointed and may feel very blessed.

A Look at Fishing and Hunting
100 Years Down the Road

I t was summer of the year 2107.

The old man walked slowly along the edge of winding stream, as he often did this time of year, his 9-year-old grandson at his side. The boy stopped often to pick up rocks along the water's edge, turning each one over to inspect it, and sometimes tossing one into the rapidly flowing river.

Suddenly the lad stopped and pointed into the water. "Look, Grandpa, there's a big fish. Can I catch it and take it home?"

The wrinkled face looked into the water at the trout and at first there was a smile. Then it turned to a saddened frown. "I'm afraid not, Eddie," came the hesitant reply. "Many years ago our country and state passed laws against catching fish. Eventually they even stopped raising young fish to release. Today there are very few in the rivers or lakes, and some species have become diseased and disappeared altogether."

"But I want to catch one," the lad insisted. "Can't I?"

"There are very large fines for taking a fish now," the grandfather explained in an ever-saddening voice. "The state and federal police are tough on illegal fishing, just as they are against all hunting ... All this used to be cared for by a Michigan Department of Natural Resources, along with conservation clubs and other habitat improvement organizations around our state. But about 50 years ago the "animal rights" groups and a bunch of so-called "do-gooders" in Congress and the State Legislature finally won out, and they put an end to all outdoor fishing and shooting sports.

"Why, nobody even raises hunting dogs anymore ... When I was a lad of your age I roamed the fields and streams, you might say with a shotgun in one hand and a fly-fishing rod in the other, and of course with my hunting dog, Queenie. Nowadays, guns and fishing rods are but relics. Unless we are a collector, we're not allowed to even own them."

"But, Grandpa," the boy answered, trying to skip yet another stone across the water, "you have many guns and fishing rods on the wall of your den."

"That's true, Eddie, and I've kept those in my collection over these many years... Some of those belonged to your great-grandfather, Steven, and even your great-great-grandfather, Ed. Several were ones I also owned as a lad. Someday they will be yours."

"But can't you show me how to fish and hunt? I want very much to do that—"

Just then the boy stopped short, his eyes fixed upon an object over his grandfather's shoulder. He pointed and remarked quietly, "Look, Grandpa, I think there's a deer at the river bend!"

The grandfather turned slowly. There at the water's edge stood a doe, and in the thicket behind her, several pair of small, pointed ears and long noses were contrasted amid the leaves.

"Be very still and watch, Eddie. That's a mama deer, a doe, and she has two young fawns behind her. If we're quiet, the fawns will come to the water to drink too."

The lad was fascinated. He'd seen pictures of deer on the laser worldnet system at school, but had been told that deer were very rare now in Michigan and throughout the United States. This was the first time he'd seen one in the wild. And, as he stood rock-still and watched, the two fawns joined the doe in the water and began to drink.

The old man and the boy looked on as the doe and her fawns quenched their thirst, and then the fawns splashed and played in the water for a brief time. Then suddenly they slipped away into the woods as quietly as they had appeared.

The old man looked long after them and finally sat down on a log near the water's edge. He placed his chin in his hand with a sigh. "It was back in 2047 when the animal rightists finally won out," he said softly, perhaps more to himself than to the boy, who by now had sat down and had begun to listen intently once more. "Many folks fought hard against them, including your great-great-grandfather, Ed, who was an outdoor writer at the time. Today, no writers or columnists dare to speak out—they'd be arrested, fined and probably even jailed if they did.

"After the new laws were passed, they first phased out the Department of Natural Resources. Then they came down hard on the Michigan United Conservation Clubs along with groups such as Pheasants Forever, The Michigan Conservation Foundation and Trout Unlimited, that had supported and paid for wildlife habitat for so many years.

"So it followed that there was no control or new propagation for wildlife. At first, some of them, the deer and turkey for example, flourished. But then disease, hard winters, and lack of maintained habitat took its toll. That's why today you see very few deer, and only a rare turkey, pheasant, rabbit or even a squirrel.

"And fish? Well, disease all but took them out too. And, with no DNR to raise fingerlings and restock the streams, they're all but non-existent today ... It's really a tragedy."

"But, Grandpa, can't we do something to bring back the wildlife, and fishing and hunting?" queried the lad.

The old man stared down the stream for a long moment, as though rejuvenating or perhaps pondering a thought he'd had many times before. Finally he answered the boy's question, almost as though talking to himself. "I believe I'll write a letter and E- mail it to all the newspapers throughout the state. Maybe this time they will listen to an old codger like—"

"But, Grandpa, you'll go to jail!"

The old man looked up at the boy then, and a smile washed over his face and his eyes began to twinkle. "I'm 85 years old, Eddie. What can they do to me? We need our wildlife and our outdoor sports back in Michigan, and we must renew the fight to get them back ... And you know, I think your great-great-grandpa Ed would want me to do this ..."